The Series on Social Emotional Learning

Teachers College Press
in partnership with the Center for Social and Emotional Education and the
Collaborative to Advance Social and Emotional Learning (CASEL)

Jonathan Cohen, *Series Editor*

CONSULTING EDITORS:
Maurice Elias, Norris M. Haynes, Roger Weissberg, and Joseph Zins

EDITORIAL ADVISORY BOARD:
J. Lawrence Aber, Diana Allensworth, Michael Ben-Avie, Robert Coles,
James P. Comer, Ann Lieberman, Pearl R. Kane, Catherine Lewis,
Karen Marschke-Tobier, John O'Neil, Nel Noddings,
Seymour B. Sarason, Thomas Sobol

How Social and Emotional Development Add Up:
Getting Results in Math and Science Education
NORRIS M. HAYNES, MICHAEL BEN-AVIE,
AND JACQUE ENSIGN, EDITORS

Higher Expectations: Promoting Social Emotional Learning
and Academic Achievement in Your School
RAYMOND J. PASI

Caring Classrooms/Intelligent Schools:
The Social Emotional Education of Young Children
JONATHAN COHEN, EDITOR

Educating Minds and Hearts:
Social Emotional Learning and the Passage into Adolescence
JONATHAN COHEN, EDITOR

Social emotional learning is now recognized as an essential aspect of children's education and a necessary feature of all successful school reform efforts. The books in this series will present perspectives and exemplary programs that foster social and emotional learning for children and adolescents in our schools, including interdisciplinary, developmental, curricular, and instructional contributions. The three levels of service that constitute social emotional learning programs will be critically presented: (1) curriculum-based programs directed to all children to enhance social and emotional competencies, (2) programs and perspectives intended for special needs children, and (3) programs and perspectives that seek to promote the social and emotional awareness and skills of educators and other school personnel.

D1081828

How Social and Emotional Development Add Up

GETTING RESULTS IN MATH AND SCIENCE EDUCATION

EDITED BY

**Norris M. Haynes, Michael Ben-Avie,
and Jacque Ensign**

Teachers College
Columbia University
New York and London

Published by Teachers College Press, 1234 Amsterdam Avenue, New York, NY 10027

Photographs by Michael Jacobson-Hardy and Laura Brooks.

Library of Congress Cataloging-in-Publication Data

How social and emotional development add up : getting results in math and science education / edited by Norris M. Haynes, Michael Ben-Avie & Jacque Ensign ; foreword by Roger P. Weissberg and Elizabeth Wright Weissberg.
    p.   cm.—(The series on social emotional learning)
Includes bibliographical references and index.
ISBN 0-8077-4307-0 (cloth : alk. paper)—ISBN 0-8077-4306-2 (pbk. : alk. paper)
    1. Mathematics—Study and teaching. 2. Science—Study and teaching. 3. Affective education. 4. Social learning. I. Haynes, Norris M. II. Ben-Avie, Michael III. Ensign, Jacque. IV. Series.

QA11.2 H68 2003
510'.71—dc21   2002075053

ISBN 0-8077-4306-2 (paper)
ISBN 0-8077-4307-0 (cloth)

Printed on acid-free paper
Manufactured in the United States of America

10 09 08 07 06 05 04 03   8 7 6 5 4 3 2 1

To
Donald J. Cohen, M.D.
Director, Yale Child Study Center
(1983–2001)

Contents

Foreword

Norris Haynes, Michael Ben-Avie, Jacque Ensign, and the other contributors to this volume are scholarly, integrative researchers and practitioners who present a compelling boundary-spanning message: Social and emotional factors play a vital role in learning math and science, both as barriers to learning and as enhancers of learning. By presenting a substantial body of empirical research and sound, engaging educational strategies, this book sets the record straight: Social and emotional variables significantly influence how children learn and how they achieve in science and math. In doing so, it establishes a landmark from which there should be no turning back. This book will positively affect the conceptualization, design, implementation, and evaluation of future social and emotional learning (SEL) programming (Elias et al., 1997; Zins, Weissberg, Wang, & Walberg, in press). It also will improve the future math and science instruction that teachers provide to students.

We appreciate that Haynes, Ben-Avie, and Ensign encouraged us, a father–daughter team, to write this foreword. As part of our collaboration, the second author agreed to share a student's perspective on how social and emotional factors have influenced her math performance, and the first author offered to share perspectives on the broader research base linking social and emotional competence to academic learning. Elizabeth Wright Weissberg wrote:

> My dad has been a major motivator throughout my life. At one point in junior high, I was having horrible trouble with math. It wasn't clicking and my teacher wasn't helping either. So every night, my dad would sit down with me and help me with my math. I wasn't always as grateful as I should have been; I sometimes got quite irritable. However, my father knew not to take it personally. I never excelled with Algebra 1, but I was able to master it with help from my father. He was what kept me going with math. Without his help, I probably would have dropped down a math level. The next year I had a wonderful math teacher. He knew exactly what he was teaching and how to teach it. Each day the lesson plan was well orga-

nized and math made complete sense. We students knew we could trust him to teach us, and if we had any questions he was there to answer them. Not one person dropped down a level from that math class. So with support from my family and teachers, I was able to push my way through the toughest math classes. I am in high school now and actually enjoying accelerated math class.

Our personal experiences reflect broader SEL-based messages that recent reviews of educational and psychological literatures offer about learning in general (Brandt, 1998; McCombs, in press; Osterman, 2000; Zins et al., in press). More specifically, they reflect the perspectives the authors of this book share about math and science learning.

A key accomplishment of this book is that it takes what is already known about the importance of social and emotional factors in learning and applies that knowledge to math and science, shedding new light on ways to help young people succeed academically. All the book's chapters, the authors state, "make the case to science and math educators that they will do their job more easily and better when youth development is part of their knowledge base and their tool kit." By following the book's clear and basic principles, and by incorporating its many examples of successful math and science instruction into their own practices, teachers are likely to see barriers to learning fall away.

The book is tremendously helpful because it goes beyond conviction and anecdote to present research findings and evidence to support what effective teachers of math and science know to be essential social and emotional components of student success:

- The students' relationship with the teacher is key. Much of the learning process involves social interaction. Students are motivated to learn (1) from teachers they respect and feel comfortable with, and (2) from competent teachers who effectively communicate their knowledge and enthusiasm about their subject matter.
- The importance of a positive, orderly classroom climate is paramount. Students learn when they experience a positive emotional climate. Children cannot learn, much less engage with challenging academic content, if classes are not well-disciplined, safe, supportive communities of learners.
- Teachers motivate students to learn better when they present organized lessons that build on current student knowledge and offer content in ways that are personally and socioculturally meaningful. Many students are easily discouraged when they are confused by

math and science concepts or see them as abstract or irrelevant to their daily lives.

- Adults' high expectations for all children, including those in lower socioeconomic settings, are critically important. Students learn best when the curriculum is appropriate for their developmental level, and they embrace challenging but achievable goals.
- The positive support of peers and family members can be as important to a student's academic success as anything that happens in the classroom.

In short, the benefit of reading this book is the awareness that a simple social and emotional equation fosters student success in math and science. It begins with the learner's own sense of himself or herself as a capable individual who can succeed in confronting challenges and solving problems, both abstract and concrete. Add to that the quality of the teacher and classroom—ideally, positive, supportive, and orderly—and a relevant, engaging, developmentally appropriate curriculum. Then consider the world outside the classroom—ideally, one in which peers and family members are enablers of learning. The sum of the parts, as this book demonstrates so well, can be the kind of successes in learning math and science that are vitally important to the well-being of our students, our schools, and our society.

Roger P. Weissberg
University of Illinois at Chicago and Collaborative for Academic,
Social, and Emotional Learning

Elizabeth Wright Weissberg
Freshman, New Trier High School

REFERENCES

Brandt, R. (1998). *Powerful learning*. Alexandria, VA: Association for Supervision and Curriculum Development.

Elias, M. J., Zins, J. E., Weissberg, R. P., Frey, K. S., Greenberg, M. T., Haynes, N. M., Kessler, R., Schwab-Stone, M. E., & Shriver, T. P. (1997). *Promoting social and emotional learning: Guidelines for educators*. Alexandria, VA: Association for Supervision and Curriculum Development.

McCombs, B. L. (in press). The learner-centered psychological principles: A framework for balancing a focus on academic achievement with a focus on social and emotional learning needs. In J. E. Zins, R. P. Weissberg, M. C. Wang, & H. J. Walberg (Eds.), *Building student success on social and emotional learning*. New York: Teachers College Press.

Osterman, K. F. (2000). Students' need for belonging in the school community. *Review of Educational Research, 70*(3), 323–367.

Zins, J. E., Weissberg, R. P., Wang, M. C., & Walberg, H. J. (Eds.). (in press). *Building student success on social and emotional learning.* New York: Teachers College Press.

Preface

STUDIES IN THE FIELDS OF EDUCATION and psychology show the significance of social and emotional factors in relationship to student learning and achievement. At a recent invitational conference at Temple University, cosponsored by the Laboratory for Student Success and the Collaborative for Academic, Social, and Emotional Learning (CASEL), a group of researchers gathered to discuss the subject, "Building School Success on Social and Emotional Learning." The conference featured the work of individuals who are actively involved in teaching social and emotional skills to students in schools across the United States. They reported on strong evidence of the impact of their interventions on students' social and emotional competence as well as school performance. Their evidence, and the evidence in this book, supports the view that addressing the social and emotional needs of students can lead to an increase in achievement motivation and in learning behaviors that, in turn, lead to an increase in academic outcomes in mathematics and science.

There are several principles that may be drawn from the chapters in this volume. By following these principles, schools in all segments of our society will be able to say, "Yes, we promote math and science achievement for everyone. In order for all our students to succeed, we attend to students' social, emotional, and cognitive development." These principles are as follows:

- Cognitive development is inextricably linked to social and emotional development.
- Social and emotional learning facilitates academic learning, and vice versa.
- Math and science education is for all children.
- Social, emotional, and contextual factors contribute significantly to children's learning and achievement in math and science.
- School climate and classroom climate contribute significantly to the development of positive attitudes and behaviors that result in strong math and science learning and high math and science achievement.
- Effective math and science teaching and learning involve approaches

that integrate strategies that help students make meaning of the processes and content of math and science by building bridges between the content of what is being taught and the life experiences of the students who are being taught.

How well children learn and perform on academic tests is influenced to a large degree by factors that have social and emotional impacts on the children. The good news is that many math and science teachers often are eager to find creative and stimulating ways to engage students' interests and to boost their performance levels. We hope that this book will contribute to those efforts.

Norris M. Haynes

Acknowledgments

We are deeply thankful to the Center for Community and School Action Research at Southern Connecticut State University for its sponsorship and support of this book.

The authors gratefully acknowledge the support of the staff of the Center for Community and School Action Research at Southern Connecticut State University (SCSU): Maureen Gilbride-Redman, M.P.A., research associate; Nnamdi Ihuegbu, university assistant; Michael Albert, M.S., university assistant; Tracie Cavanaugh, university assistant; Wanda Harris, M.Ed., M.P.A.; Susan Tiso, program manager; Karen Doepper, program assistant. We appreciate the unwavering encouragement and support of Dr. Rodney Lane, dean of the School of Education at SCSU. We also thank Dr. Joy E. Fopiano, coordinator of the School Psychology Program at SCSU, who encouraged and provided motivational support for this project.

We thank Myra Cleary for superb copy editing. We also thank Brian Ellerbeck and Lyn Grossman of Teachers College Press.

We are inspired by the work of our colleagues at the Collaborative for Academic, Social, and Emotional Learning. We extend our sincere thanks to Dr. Roger P. Weissberg, Executive Director of CASEL. Members of the Social and Emotional Learning Book Series editorial group provided helpful review and critique. They include Drs. Jonathan Cohen, Roger Weissberg, Maurice Elias, and Joseph Zins. Norris Haynes extends a special thanks to Drs. Timothy Shriver and Roger Weissberg, who have been steadfast in their encouragement, support, and friendship over the years.

A special thanks to Isabel Stein, consulting editor, who read many of the early drafts of this book and offered insightful comments that helped us write the book that we really wanted to write.

We thank our families, especially our children who have inspired us and who have been patient, understanding, and supportive of us as we labored to produce this book.

Jacque Ensign would like to convey her appreciation to the staff of the Yale University Child Study Center's School Development Program, who warmly welcomed her when she became a visiting professor. She also thanks the teachers and principals who welcomed her and her teacher education students into their classrooms in New Haven, and offers special thanks to Kathy Jones, Ann Traiz, and Teassie Blassingame.

Finally, we are deeply grateful to the late Donald Cohen, M.D., former director of the Yale Child Study Center, whose legacy and spirit continue to inspire us to speak loudly on behalf of the well-being of all children around the world.

We thank Linda Brouard for her masterful help in getting this manuscript into shape and for her humor.

Michael Ben-Avie recalls: This book originated during a meeting at Teachers College Press (TCP) about five years ago. Faye Zucker, then editor at TCP and today executive editor at Corwin Press, had called the meeting to discuss a new book series on social and emotional education. Norris Haynes and I attended the meeting as representatives of the Yale Child Study Center. I recall saying at one point, "I don't want to do a book on social and emotional development—I want to do a book on math and science." Startled, everyone turned to me. I tried to explain that if we could articulate how social and emotional development are related to math and science learning, then we would have something truly innovative and powerful to say. We are deeply indebted to Faye Zucker, who recognized the potential of this idea. Her enthusiasm for this book sustained our efforts over the years.

Social and Emotional Development in Relation to Math and Science Learning—An Introduction to the Argument

Michael Ben-Avie, Norris M. Haynes, Jacque Ensign, & Trudy Raschkind Steinfeld

WHAT ARE WE GOING TO DO about mathematics and science education? Throughout the country, caring and talented educators are frustrated and puzzled. Since the Third International Mathematics and Science Study (TIMSS), there has been more and more focus on this subject: In response, many educators have made creative and valuable contributions that range from the global (systemic reform) to the specific (innovative ways to use new materials in the classroom). Even so, students' willingness and ability to learn, retain, recall, and apply math and science concepts and facts have not improved nearly as fast, or as much, as was expected or as is urgently needed.

We often say, "If what you're doing isn't working, do something different." But which different thing should educators do? Many of the new ways of presenting these subjects and many of the staff development reforms are excellent. Recently, the something different has been raising the bar of accountability for high performance. Yet, that attempted solution may now have become part of the problem because the anxiety at all levels from pre-K classrooms to superintendents' offices has risen as the bar has risen. And people don't think clearly or do their best work when they're anxious. Discussions of anxiety and motivation are usually prominent topics in a book about social and emotional development. Less so in a book about math and science.

In planning this book, we realized that if we could articulate how social and emotional development are related to math and science learning, then we would have something truly innovative and powerful to say. We knew this had not been done, and at the time did not pause to wonder why not. We still are not sure that we have the answer, although we are fortunate that our colleagues in the Collaborative for Academic, Social, and Emotional Learning are now addressing this very subject. In fact, they perceive it as being so important that they recently changed their own name (which has previously been the Collaborative to Advance Social and Emotional Learning). This book, therefore, is part of a far-reaching effort. In this book, the authors provide different entry points into the discussion. We will have achieved our desired outcome if this book sparks discussions on (1) the nature of the relationship, and (2) how we may promote each one through the other.

At first glance, the premise of this book may seem like a paradox: The way to improve math and science learning at this point is to widen, not narrow, our focus, to include social and emotional development as necessary components of student learning. The authors in this book want all adults who work with children and youth to recognize that students' ability to learn is inextricably connected with their development as human beings. Expressing this premise using math and science language, we could say, for example, (1) that learning correlates directly with healthy, full development, and (2) that healthy, full development potentiates and is the catalyst for learning. The converse of these statements is also true. When development is constrained or incomplete, it's as if we were multiplying fractions and getting ever-decreasing proportions as the result: Inadequate attempts at learning by a student whose development is uneven yield only tiny proportions of accomplishment, accompanied by ever-increasing frustration and expectation of failure. And because students who are not developing well tend to be distracted, depressed, irritable, and worse, constrained development also raises the threshold at which learning can occur so high that it seems as if no amount of energy in the system is sufficient to reach that threshold.

The whole, learning, developing student is present at all times. Therefore both educators and youth developers must widen their focus and widen their area of expertise. The authors make the case to science and math educators that they will do their job more easily and better when youth development is part of their knowledge base and their tool kit. They also make the case to youth developers that they will serve students better when they themselves know more about math and science concepts, facts, and applications and are better able to support the teaching of these subjects in schools.

The authors have ample substantiation for the book's premise. Research shows that school communities actually do promote both learning and development when they apply knowledge of youth development to the math and science curriculum, the schedule of the school day, the math and science activities and classroom discourse, personal relationships, discussions of individual children and classes, and ways of assessing student learning (Comer, Ben-Avie, Haynes, & Joyner, 1999). Furthermore, there is no question that when students are succeeding academically, many potential social and emotional problems are avoided, and students are far more likely to become successful adults in their community.

In the opening chapter ("Youth Development and Student Learning in Math and Science") Ben-Avie, Haynes, and colleagues make two arguments. First, for the same reasons that a low-performing middle school cannot suddenly expect that, tomorrow, all its eighth-grade students will be able to start to study advanced algebra, teachers cannot just say one day that all students will work well in teams and reason well in class. The students may not be socially and emotionally ready to take risks, speak out in class, offer ideas for the group to consider, or initiate a new line of reasoning. Students who rarely have been asked to offer conjectures will long for the procedures and concrete computations that clearly guide their actions. If we are to help students move from a state of unreadiness to a state of readiness to conjecture, reason, and defend mathematical ideas, we must have in-depth knowledge of who the students are and what their experiences are in other classrooms and settings. In helping to promote the students' transition, math and science teachers cannot rely only on knowledge of their own academic disciplines. They also need knowledge of youth development.

Second, social problem-solving skills are related to cognitive problem-solving skills. This argument is based on research that we have designed and conducted. For example, we found in one of our studies that the strength of the relationship between students' social knowledge of themselves and others and their achievement in mathematics was very strong. The relationship found in that study between social competence and achievement in math suggests a convergence in problem-solving skills—both in tackling tough social situations and succeeding in them and in tackling and solving cognitive problems in math.

Other studies cited in the same chapter reveal several important predictors of students' academic perseverance, which we define as students' persistence in performing strategic behaviors that increase the likelihood of academic success, regardless of obstacles or distractions. In the order of their importance in our findings, these predictors were (1) students' ability to quickly recover their healthiest sense of self during and after challenging social situations (we call this coping), (2) students' feelings of efficacy when solving challenging problems in mathematics and science (we call this problem solving in math and science), and (3) students' tendency to trust adults and to develop supportive relationships with them (we call this engagement with adults). These four variables—academic perseverance, coping, problem solving in math and science, and engagement with adults—appear throughout the chapter and are echoed in subsequent chapters in this book.

John Zeuli and Michael Ben-Avie (Chapter 2, "Connecting with Students on a Social and Emotional Level Through In-Depth Discussions of Mathematics") argue that teachers need to start where the children are in order to help them ultimately master the content and skills that have relevance in the larger world. How do teachers learn where the children are? Prolonged observation is one important way. Being mentored by other adults who are well educated about child development is another way. Perhaps the most effective way is by communicating directly with—and listening fully to—the children. The teachers reported on in this chapter who most closely approximated the reform ideal were the ones who learned about the children through in-depth discussions with them about mathematical concepts. In this way, teachers are able to deliver high-quality lessons while supporting their students' social and emotional development as individual learners and as members of a community of learners.

Veronica Roberts (Chapter 3, "Mathematics and Science Readiness and Policy") profiles work done in an urban school district. When well-prepared teachers and challenging curricula are used, she reports, even low-income students succeed. High expectations and quality teaching for all students are particularly critical to success among low-income minority students. Roberts knows that these students consistently meet high performance standards when given the right learning conditions. Educators and parents alike must begin to have expectations of high standards for disadvantaged students. They must foster the development of children's confidence in their own ability to excel in algebra, geometry, and calculus as well as the physical and life sciences. In turn, students must know that we expect them to master mathematics and science learning well enough to earn college degrees in the fields of mathematics, science, and technology.

Some authors in this book (see Ben-Avie et al. in Chapter 1, Roberts in Chapter 3, and Bippert and Bezuk in Chapter 4, "Developmental Pathways to Mathematics Achievement") discuss the Yale School Development

Program, which has been one of the leading school improvement programs proven to have successfully addressed the social and emotional developmental needs of all students (and particularly students from difficult life circumstances) while enhancing their academic growth and achievement outcomes. Those authors describe the application of the Comer Process to math and science teaching and learning. They demonstrate that learning occurs best when math and science teachers have a holistic sense of the child being taught and build their instruction on that foundation. Other authors share specific classroom-based programs that have been designed to integrate and respond to the experiences of culturally diverse students. The evidence suggests that many of these programs do make a significant difference in the math and science achievement and test performance of socially and emotionally challenged students, in large measure due to the attention, sensitivity, and carefully designed experiential activities that they include.

Judy Bippert and Nadine Bezuk (Chapter 4) specifically discuss developmental pathways to math and science achievement in classrooms when students play math games. They share the basic notion from James Comer's work that the social context in schools and classrooms influences and even determines how well and how effectively teachers teach and students learn. Bippert and Bezuk describe studies that were conducted in San Diego, their school district. They cite Borton, Preston, and Bippert (1996), who presented data showing that students' improvement in mathematics achievement may be predicted by their sense of caring teachers who maintain high expectations for learning and a well-disciplined classroom. The authors also describe a longitudinal study (Borton, Preston, & Bippert, 1998) that looked at implementation of the Comer Process and student academic success. This study involved 12 schools, which serve approximately 11,500 students, have diverse student populations, and are in different geographic communities. In their analysis of the data, they observed that continued, significant efforts by schools to improve school climate, parent involvement, and teacher efficacy are important components in any strategy to improve student achievement in math.

In Chapter 5 ("Success for Minority Students in Mathematics and Science: Prerequisites for Excellence and Equity"), Dionne Jones notes the distinctive requirements for teaching low-income African American and Hispanic students. While all children benefit from having adequately prepared classrooms and teachers and relevant subject matter, there are students who often are not given such benefits. By citing examples of successful programs, Jones demonstrates what a difference such benefits make in students' math and science achievement.

Jacque Ensign (Chapter 6, "Nurturing Mathematics Learning in the

Classroom") describes her work with teachers in inner-city classrooms. She shows that students are turned on to learning and problem solving in math when a math problem or a science experiment incorporates elements of the students' life experience. Math and science formulas are not just memorized in the abstract without being connected to something meaningful. They are considered in contexts that are familiar and are related to facts that are germane. Students who often have not been successful in mathematics experience a heightened sense of efficacy when they realize they are experts at solving problems involving mathematics or science in their everyday lives and that they can apply those strategies to solving math problems in school. The student internalizes the information, connects with it, and responds not just cognitively but socially and emotionally. Students feel respected and heard when their teachers solicit and use their life experiences. This helps them trust their teachers and engage in developing relationships with them. In addition, this helps students to take risks with their peers and teachers and to learn healthy coping skills as they learn how to accept and deal with differences when revealing details about their everyday lives.

Ensign's chapter also sparks the question of what specific structural changes are needed if the U.S. educational system is to promote child development and student learning. Schools of education could become the most effective leverage point. However, today preservice administrators and teachers generally are required to take only a course or two on child development; their academic program is largely lacking courses leading to an understanding of child development. To effectively promote child development and student learning, teacher education programs will have to revamp how they teach courses and, indeed, how the programs themselves are organized. Rather than isolating courses on child development, courses on learning will have to be closely tied to or even taught collaboratively with child development courses. Besides theory, teachers need to experience the close relationship between development and learning.

David Pettigrew and James Dolan (Chapter 7, "Excellence and Equity: A Regional Consortium for Reforming Science Education") also focus on the power of partnerships, in this case a regional consortium that was launched at Southern Connecticut State University. The authors describe how a university helps teachers learn to develop new ways of learning. Rather than being taught about hands-on learning, these teachers learn science by doing, and then are supported as they help their own students learn by doing. They recommend that courses and inservice programs include a focus on how teachers' learning is tied to teachers' own development. After all, if teachers become better aware of how their own development and learning are integrally related, they may be more able to appreciate the value of addressing their students' development and learning as integrally connected.

Pettigrew and Dolan also introduce the topic of excellence and equity into our consideration of how social and emotional development are related to math and science learning. They explain that systemic reform in science education is as much about science as it is about engendering skills and attitudes related to inquiry, collaboration, communication, respect for diversity, and social responsibility. The new standards, they show, emphasize that "science is often a collaborative endeavor, and all science depends on the ultimate sharing and debating of ideas."

Mary Moran and Michael Ben-Avie (Chapter 8, "Stretching Students' Future Orientation") contribute to the discussion by describing an intervention that focused on stretching students' future orientation. Over the course of several years, Moran and her colleagues helped students envision themselves as future college students, helped them understand the process and inherent organization of tasks involved in applying to college, and then provided a structure in which they could successfully perform those tasks. In creating a well-supervised extracurricular youth development group, Moran and her colleagues created a cadre of young people who bonded with, looked after, and encouraged one another. As the students developed and used their new skills to imagine and prepare for a better future, they rededicated themselves to their academic work in high school: The graduation rate among Moran's group of students was 93%, whereas the national average at the time was 74%, and the average for students from their city (Houston) was only 52%.

Tim Fowler (Chapter 9, "A Corporate Partner in the Science Classroom") approaches the topic of the relationship between social and emotional development in relation to math and science learning from an interesting perspective: He has a Ph.D. in molecular biology and is currently obtaining a master's degree in teaching at Seattle University. His argument takes off from a point that we make in the opening chapter about partnerships. He suggests that educating children and youth to be socially and emotionally well and to succeed academically is a collective task that all adults and community institutions must share. Meaningful partnerships involving people who are committed to positive change in children's lives and in their learning can have far-reaching implications for success in math and science learning. Teachers cannot do it alone. They require the support and commitment of partnerships to make significant improvements in students' learning in math and science as well as social and emotional growth. Fowler argues that integrating the high school classroom and the biotechnology company can have a powerful, positive effect on student social and emotional development. Thus, corporations willing to open their doors to students have the potential to impact the whole developmental trajectory of students' lifepaths.

In this book, the authors suggest that many underachieving students are socially and emotionally challenged due to life circumstances over which they have little or no control, and often their academic performance reflects the negative impact of these difficult life circumstances. Schools offer them the best hope for rising above these circumstances and developing into successful, well-adjusted adults. The international math and science studies that compare U.S. students with students from around the world do not include social and emotional indices that reflect differences in life challenges faced by U.S. students in comparison to their international counterparts. One would imagine that if U.S. schools and classrooms could be more effective in helping students adjust well to school despite the many social and emotional challenges they face outside school, the results of the international math and science studies would be much different.

REFERENCE

Comer, J. P., Ben-Avie, M., Haynes, N. M., & Joyner, E. T. (1999). *Child by child: The Comer process for change in education*. New York: Teachers College Press.

CHAPTER 1

Youth Development and Student Learning in Math and Science

Michael Ben-Avie, Norris M. Haynes, Jayne White,
Jacque Ensign, Trudy Raschkind Steinfeld,
Loleta D. Sartin, & David A. Squires

OUR INTEREST IN THE RELATIONSHIP between youth development and student learning has led us to study educational and psychological interventions designed by nonprofit, government, and corporate partnerships. Our research has shown that paying attention to students' development does not detract from student learning. In fact, promoting the highest levels of development among students seems to be what helps them reach high academic goals.

In response to the performance of U.S. students in the Third International Mathematics and Science Study (TIMSS), there have been calls for higher standards, better instruction, and tougher assessments. We believe that the real question is not how to create higher standards. *The real question is how to help schools implement programs that will meet the already high standards.* Yet, we are confronted with an overcrowded curriculum that no longer serves either students' developmental needs or their learning needs. How can schools possibly focus successfully on both?

Many schools throughout the country believe that they are taking youth development into account by teaching a "developmentally appropriate" curriculum. We have found that merely packaging a curriculum in terms of "ages and stages" does not actually address the true developmental needs of students. A course or two on child development in graduate school is helpful in learning about the discipline of youth development, but it is not sufficient to ensure that teachers will routinely act in ways that promote students' development. Schools concerned about promoting children's development have added social skills programs, after-school programs, and health clinics—yet they have not considered touching the core academic mission of the school. Nor have they designed ways to use the curriculum to impact students' developmental trajectories.

Young people need to have some sense of where they're going, what they want for themselves, their responsibilities to other people, and their responsibilities to the larger society. The day after the results of the Third International Mathematics and Science Study (TIMSS) were released in 1996, James P. Comer, founder of the Yale School Development Program, said that learning the formulas and procedures of mathematics and the sciences is essential, but knowing only formulas and procedures will not help the young make sense of our rapidly changing world. They need an education that will enable them to handle technology, the sciences, and all the contradictions that are involved in the social world—to empathize with and care about people who are not as successful as they are. Today's students need an education that trains them to assess, decide, and act in ways that are good for themselves and society—and this requires that their teachers continuously demonstrate their knowledge not only of math and science but also of social and emotional development.

This chapter is based on two related premises: (1) Students can learn more effectively if their development and their social and emotional learning are reflected in teaching strategies and the curriculum, and (2) those who are concerned with promoting the social and emotional well-being of children need to learn the nuts and bolts of teaching math and science. Too often, programs designed to promote students' social and emotional learning do not take into account students' major job in their lives: to study, learn, and successfully use the information and notions taught in their academic courses. There is a strong relationship between student learning and youth development, including social and emotional aspects of development. The school schedule is a tool that schools may use to spark developmental experiences, the outcome of a process that aligns and balances curricular units with students' developmental needs (more about this later). Developmental experiences stretch students' future orientation, which we understand as the ability to conceive of one's own development. Thus, continuing academic learning and youth development lead to increasingly accurate self-awareness and resourcefulness in all situations, in school and in the wider world outside.

STUDENTS' LEARNING IN MATH AND SCIENCE IS RELATED TO THEIR SOCIAL AND EMOTIONAL LEARNING

At the Yale Child Study Center, our Impact Analysis and Strategies Group (IASG)[1] conducts research on educational and psychological interventions designed by nonprofit, government, and corporate partnerships. While looking for other things, we repeatedly have uncovered links between social competence in tough situations and achievement in math. For example, we administered the Behavior Assessment Schedule for Students (BASS) (Haynes, 1995) to a total of 831 middle school students in School Development Program schools. BASS is designed to measure students' self-reported thinking and beliefs about their social interactions and problems. We also obtained the students' achievement scores in mathematics. The strength of the relationship between students' social knowledge of themselves and others and their achievement in mathematics was found to be strong.[2] This makes sense. In both math and social interactions, success depends on awareness of the challenge and of an ideal outcome, skills to map out a strategy to solve the problem, and willingness and skill in persisting at and refining the strategy until a positive outcome is achieved. (Summaries of our foundational studies appear in the appendix to this chapter.)

If we can show the nature of the relationship between youth development and student learning, then we can guide those who are intervening in the lives of children to help children succeed in learning math and science. With a better understanding of this relationship we should be able to clarify whether individual students are not achieving in math and science because of youth development issues or because of math and science issues. Most important, we should be able to guide public policy regarding how to improve the quality of education for all students.

The act of learning is described by Jerome Bruner. In *The Process of Education* (1977), Bruner reports on the Woods Hole gathering of some 35 scientists, scholars, and educators who came together for 10 days in September 1959 to discuss how education in science might be improved. Bruner discusses the act of learning and notes:

> Learning a subject seems to involve three almost simultaneous processes:
>   1. Acquisition of new information—often information that runs counter to or is a replacement for what the person has previously known implicitly or explicitly.
>   2. Transformation—the process of manipulating knowledge to make it fit new tasks.
>   3. Evaluation—checking whether the way we have manipulated information is adequate to the task. (p. 48)

How child development and student learning are related has been a topic of heated debate since the early years of the past century: Is child development independent of learning? Is learning actually development? Are learning and development mutually dependent and interactive processes? Or does learning awaken development? (Vygotsky, 1978). How Vygotsky apparently viewed the relationship between learning and development is explained by Eric Bredo (1997), who uses the metaphor of a tennis game: "*Learning* might involve improving one's forehand return in tennis, while *development* would involve being able to place elements of this act in the context of the likely reactions of one's opponent" (p. 38, emphasis in original).

Students' development may be balanced, constrained, or uneven depending on the way students understand their experiences. In optimal circumstances, that understanding is guided by skilled and caring adults who are available and accessible at critical moments. Development is usually constrained when the student has physical or psychological needs that aren't met. When development is uneven, there is an overemphasis on one aspect of development to the detriment of overall development in the present and, possibly, in the future. To illustrate the latter, if students' cognitive development has been overemphasized to the detriment of their social development, they may be at grade level in their learning of math and science, but may be unable to successfully engage in teamwork and group problem solving, which ultimately may impact their success at higher levels of mathematics.

Mature adult development is expressed through, among other things, professional conduct, participation in groups or networks in which people exchange thoughts and ideas, and a sense of one's place along one's lifepath. At each point along the lifepath, one's desirable human functioning is defined through reflecting on what one has learned from past experiences and orienting oneself to the future. In adult development, desirable human functioning includes taking care of oneself and family, personal control, respecting the rights and needs of other people, responsible citizenship, productive employment, and taking advantage of appropriate opportunities. Development is an unending, incremental process that continues throughout an individual's life. (In our research, we discuss youth development and student learning in terms of competencies. See the appendix to this chapter for definitions of the youth development variables—competencies—that we measure in our surveys.)

When the school is a healthy place for adults and students, students begin to see themselves as part of a collective set of thoughts and actions. They develop the sense of security that they need to try out their ideas, to puzzle through new concepts, and to grow and identify with increasingly larger groups.

Consider students' participation in classroom discussions. If students are not readily participating, is it because of a math and science issue or a youth development issue? For example, the process of seeking truth includes experiences such as going out on a limb to confront distortions and misconceptions and to challenge known facts. For classrooms to nurture the open-minded, skeptical, and self-critical disposition of the scientist, classroom communities must be anchored in healthy relationships so that students will be willing to take risks and also won't perceive their teachers' efforts to correct their thinking as punitive. The learning process can be painful when assumptions are held up to the test of the scientific method. A classroom imbued with respect and trust enables the student to engage in this process with the knowledge that insights will be given attention and errors will not be publicly or privately ridiculed. A respectful tone of voice, respect due to one's elders, and the respect given to differing viewpoints do not naturally unfold among students, but must be modeled and learned.

(In a classroom riddled with mistrust and disrespect, the budding scientists' healthy skepticism could be misinterpreted as insolence. Consequently, inquisitive students could be barred from engaging in scientific debate and shy students might hold back, lacking a taste for that debate.)

Knowledge of youth development enables us to see that supportive relationships enhance students' engagement and motivate students to continue to study and learn. Whenever instructional activities in math and science become too abstract, whenever students become disinterested and disillusioned, the generative relationships that students have with others—and with their own selves—have the power to sustain them in the learning process. Gradually, they can reorganize their everyday experiences under the rubric of mathematical and scientific concepts (see Vygotsky, 1978), incorporating ever more abstract notions in this incremental way.

Schools should be healing places—places in which adults promote students' attainment of the highest levels of development without stigmatizing youth whose development is uneven. Healthy youth development and student learning are more likely in a school community in which all the adults provide a place that is predictable and a model for all future relationships.

THE RELATIONSHIP BETWEEN LEARNING AND DEVELOPMENT: DEVELOPMENTAL EXPERIENCES

Developmental experiences are the building blocks of young people's competencies and worldview. They are characterized by (1) cognitive processing that leads to a sense of well-being that, in turn, promotes future interest (J.P. Comer, personal communication, 1998), and (2) a reorientation of the self into a larger context. Even though the process at first may be painful, developmental experiences eventually produce a sense of psychological pleasure as the individual realizes that he or she can deal with conflict and/or handle the increased choices of how and what to think and feel and how to behave in this larger context.

Activities provide the spark or trigger, and the students' self-awareness provides the proof of whether an experience has been developmental: When students think about, are able to write about, and express what they derived from the activity and response (what they are now able to do with this new learning), then the activity can be considered to be one that promotes a developmental experience.

Our research shows that when adults intervene appropriately in children's lifepaths, they are setting up the conditions for developmental experiences to occur.

Young people also may have negative developmental experiences:

those that limit choices for thoughts, feelings, and behavior. Experiences such as being told to mouth the words instead of being taught how to carry a tune, or being told to go home and study longer and harder instead of being taught specific strategies for studying more effectively and efficiently, are negative developmental experiences. These experiences lead to worldviews in which others can sing, but "I am tone deaf," or others can do math, but "I am stupid," each of which is an identity label that tends to limit future positive development.

Youth development is a continuum of growth, of acts of learning, and of experiences of self-awareness that become part of the structure of the young person's lifepath. As on a hiking path, at each step along one's lifepath one can look back, look to all sides, look to one's footing, look up, and look ahead. At any point, one may have a wide or a constricted view of where one has been, what one has been through, and where one is going. And like a hiking path, the lifepath can take a turn that opens a new vista. When one takes or makes a lifepath turn, one is reorienting one's thinking and perceiving oneself in a larger context that offers more choices for thoughts, feelings, and behaviors. This is the definition of a developmental experience.

It is the responsibility of all who work with young people to show them how to recognize, or create, and to handle these turns on their lifepaths so that these developmental experiences are positive. In doing so, we help them to acquire, transform, and evaluate their knowledge of themselves and their potential. This knowledge is of the strengths and skills they already possess, of situations and people that help them grow and learn, and of accomplishments that will mark their maturation into responsible, self-sustaining members of healthy communities. Developmental experiences stretch students' future orientation, which is both a belief system and, in the words of William T. Brown, a postdoctoral fellow at the Yale Child Study Center, the ability to conceive of one's own development.

A developmental experience—the reorientation toward oneself and the subject matter—can come in a sudden upwelling of insight, or it can be a slower or different type of development that virtually assembles itself before the student or teacher becomes consciously aware of the change. The way our schools are organized, students and teachers tend to be rewarded primarily for quick, and sometimes incomplete, responses. Opportunities for the slower (and often richer) responses are rare.

Role of Schools

Schools promote students' development by ensuring that school activities and assignments are developmental experiences that are relevant to the students' lives and also relevant to the math and scientific concepts that are being taught. Teachers reinforce this when they help students to think through each activity. Such an orientation and curriculum have the added benefit of helping students to develop the habit of perceiving their failures in a new light: as opportunities to get more information about their current learning strategies. From this information they and their adult guides can tailor new, personalized strategies for successful learning, retaining, and recalling, without slipping into negative self-images and self-talk (Anderson, 1981; Dilts, 1998, 1999; O'Connor & Seymour, 1990).

An example of fashioning such a personalized strategy is the following typical scenario: The teacher and student unpackage what, specifically, the student is currently doing—and in what sequence—when starting to study for a test. Together they discover that as the student contemplates studying, he sags and says to himself, "What's the use? I never get good grades anyway." Then he closes his books and takes a long nap, waking up too anxious to study but too well rested to sleep. He takes the test underprepared, anxious, and fatigued.

After repeating the student's comments in a way that lets him know he has been heard without being judged, the teacher guides the student to take a "trip into the future" to a time when the student already has had plenty of experience studying well and receiving good grades. The teacher uses postures, gestures, tones of voice, a tempo, and specific sensory words that best suit the student's most desired feeling state in this imaginary future ("Notice how you're standing, now that you have learned some ways to perform well on a test." "Look at your reflection in a mirror, and see how cheerful you can let yourself look now that you're happier with yourself for making progress." "Notice the words of encouragement you give yourself that get your energy up and remind you to use your new strategies.").

In order for the student to imagine this fully, his feeling state must change, for that is the nature of the connection between mind and body. In this new state, the student is more open to learning the new strategy, which is a highly visual memorization process that allows him to know for sure that he can store and retrieve the information on which he will be tested. The teacher and student practice that memorization strategy over the course of several meetings, and also reinforce the sense of the student's movement toward that future time when being a competent, confident student is part of his self-identity. Before each test, the teacher and student exchange a signal they've agreed on that reminds the student that he is in the process of moving toward this better future. Not only is this hand-tailoring of a strategy helpful for achieving better grades, but it is also a developmental experience because the student is learning to assess his own movement along his lifepath and to recognize that he has the capacity to imagine a better future and develop the skills to achieve it.

Intervening in the Lifepaths of Students

The more students' current lifepaths lead them toward limited options, the more urgent is the need for adults to consciously design positive developmental experiences that:

- Include access to settings and people the students typically would not have encountered or would have encountered only on a limited basis
- Are of sufficient intensity and duration
- Promote their belonging in a group
- Are likely to stretch their sense of their orientation toward their own future and the future in general

For school staff, taking a developmental perspective means recognizing that students (and colleagues): (1) are who they are and do what they do as a result of the developmental experiences that they have had since birth, and (2) are becoming who they will be in part as a result of the experiences they are having right now under that staff person's influence.

Young people develop the motivation to achieve in school and in life through their interactions with adults as they navigate through school, home, work, and recreational activities. However, not all learning is constructive—consider Dewey's (1938) famous example of the individual who starts out on a career of burglary and through practice becomes a highly expert burglar. Hence the importance of a student's personal engagement with a positive role model, the teacher.

The teacher is the carrier of the value of academic learning. As an authority figure in the mind of the child, the teacher is able to frame the learning and reframe students' energy from negative to positive, outcome-oriented thoughts, feelings, and behavior. James Comer, our mentor at the Yale Child Study Center and founder of the Yale School Development Program, told us that once students have internalized the value of academic learning—once they have made the learning their own—they derive three rewards: personal fulfillment, a sense of achievement and competence, and knowledge that is useful in the world. Until students make learning their own, they need to be engaged with an authority figure who values learning. The relationship is important because it fosters students' emotional attachment to the knowledge.

Another way in which schools intervene in the lifepaths of the students is through using the school schedule to spark developmental experiences, which are more likely to occur when curricular units are aligned and balanced with students' developmental needs.

TURNING THE SCHOOL SCHEDULE INTO A TOOL
TO SPARK DEVELOPMENTAL EXPERIENCES:
THE BALANCED CURRICULUM PROCESS

Guilford County Schools in North Carolina implemented the balanced curriculum process designed by the Yale School Development Program's David Squires, one of the authors of this chapter. In 1993, three formerly independent school systems—Greensboro, High Point, and Guilford County—merged. The new school district's first superintendent, Jerry Weast, implemented the School Development Program throughout the system.

The following is a description of how a school in Guilford County school district used the School Development Program to balance the curriculum. The initial push for this came from both the superintendent and the principal, who were at first concerned about test scores. They decided that they would take a look at the math program since they had a pretty good sense about what needed to be done, and were considering a number of different options. They wanted to do an after-school program so students could receive math tutoring, and they wanted to provide a "problem a day" for everybody to work on. However, they also knew that the real problem was that the teachers had not had conversations about what is most important to teach in math. Both the superintendent and principal had examined the math textbooks and had had conversations about them. They found that in the math books the concepts were presented in half a page and the rest of the page was filled with problems. There wasn't really enough depth there, they concluded. In addition, there were so many topics that it was difficult to get the depth that was needed. The message this sent to the teachers was: We want you to cover all of these topics, but you are never going to have enough time to cover any of them in depth so that students really will understand the concepts of fractions or multiplication or measurements. The principal and the superintendent were also concerned because they knew that the standardized test did not necessarily reinforce the good teaching of math. They knew that the fill-in-the-bubble, one-out-of-four-you-could-guess method wasn't going to do the trick. Although they probably could push the teachers to do more of that, they knew it would unbalance the curriculum.

The superintendent and the principal asked, "How do we improve our existing math programs?" and decided to use the balanced curriculum process. This process is a form of staff development in which the children and their development are kept in clear focus while staff members define, re-envision, and rearrange what is taught and when it is taught so that it reinforces academic mastery and youth development. Staff also examine the standards, the textbooks, and the assessments, and use the results of unit and standardized assessments to help improve math and science results. In middle and high schools, students may be part of the balancing process.

A balanced curriculum for a school district or school is the product of a threefold process: (1) defining, re-envisioning, and rearranging; (2) aligning and balancing; and (3) assessing.

Defining, Re-envisioning, and Rearranging the Preexisting Curriculum

Teachers and administrators in all grade levels work together to define the preexisting curriculum with an eye toward eliminating repetition and gaining more time to teach what the larger school community considers important. Teachers decide how much of their own ideas and professional expertise should be mixed with the views of other experts in the field as they discuss their perceptions of students' developmental needs, the existing curriculum and instructional program, the textbooks, national standards, district/state goals and frameworks, and the content and format of standardized tests. Then they redistribute the math and science units and rethink what to put in each unit and the amount of time the unit would take. The result of their work is a coherent, multiyear curriculum that has a wide scope and a clear sequence.

Aligning and Balancing the Curriculum with National and State Standards and with Standardized Assessments

Aligning and balancing the curriculum are necessary to address two faulty assumptions: (1) teaching the text leads to good results on tests; and (2) teachers naturally cover the content of tests in their classrooms. When the curriculum is aligned and balanced, classroom activities adhere to state standards, national professional association standards, local standards, standardized tests, state tests, local tests, and the six developmental pathways that James P. Comer has identified as critical to academic learning (physical, cognitive, psychological, language, social, and ethical).

Assessing the New Curriculum

An aligned and balanced curriculum provides the framework for considering assessment issues. A new curriculum is always something of a gamble. School communities are betting that if students successfully complete the unit activities, they will do well on unit assessments. If students do well on unit assessments, teachers are betting that they will do well on the standardized assessments for the state. To figure out whether the bet has been

won, the balanced curriculum process systematizes data-collection procedures so that schools can determine whether students' unit scores predict
scores on standardized test-item clusters. Teachers and administrators
come to a consensus about how data from unit assessments will be collected, reported, and aggregated.

Later, if results from standardized tests are not up to expectations,
teachers and administrators can return to the grid; identify units and activities aligned with the deficient skill areas; and modify, realign, and rebal-
ance them to strengthen instruction for the next year. The cycle ensures
continuous improvement in the curriculum using data-driven decision
making.

KNOWLEDGE OF YOUTH DEVELOPMENT PROMOTES
SUSTAINED COMMITMENT

School communities also promote students' developmental experiences
when they tailor interventions that are designed in accordance with principles of youth development. One such principle is that development is an
incremental process. Because development is incremental, it is helpful to
see any experience as a potential developmental experience and to see each
developmental experience as part of an ongoing flow, rather than as a one-
time "Eureka!" event. Thus, common sense suggests that if we intervene in
the lives of middle school students, then we should continue the intervention at least until they graduate from high school. Yet, this type of sustained commitment is rare. One notable exception has been the Institute
for Student Achievement (ISA), which Ben-Avie, Steinfeld, and colleagues
evaluated for 3 years.

The ISA was founded in 1990 by Gerard and Lilo Leeds, cofounders
of CMP Media Inc. ISA is a not-for-profit public/private venture in Man-
hasset, New York. Its self-described mission is "to improve the quality of
education for children and youth at risk so that they can succeed in our
society." Gerard Leeds has a persuasive argument to justify the expenditure
necessary to attempt this: Provide integrated school-based academic and
counseling support services to students identified as being at risk of dropping out of school, at a cost of $3,000 to $5,000 per student annually—
approximately $20,000 for a 4–6-year program—and eventually "society
gets its money back every two years for the working life of each person."
In Leeds's words, "When [ISA students] graduate from college, they'll be
making $30,000 to $40,000 a year. They'll average paying $10,000 a year
in taxes. When they graduate from college, in two years they'll have paid
society back in taxes" (quoted in Fischler, 1998, p. 25). Furthermore, soci-

ety saves by "avoiding the future costs of unemployment, health and welfare support and the costs of the criminal justice system" (p. 25).

ISA's experience teaches us that if you want to make a difference in the lives of children, you can't jump in and out of their lives. You also can't expect major changes in the trajectories of children's lives after only a year or so of intervention. ISA provides school-based academic enrichment and counseling support services to middle and high school students who have been identified as most likely to drop out. It provides the students with easy access to adults who help them manage their anger, resolve interpersonal conflicts with teachers and other students, and deal with other issues that may interfere with their learning. Whereas other interventions are coordinated by a single individual, ISA brings in a team to support the students. This team approach helps students to maintain a sense of continuity of relationships when individual team members are promoted or leave. ISA's team approach carries over to the students: Students affiliate with ISA as if it were a youth group. Whereas many after-school interventions provide students with academic reinforcement and enrichment, ISA's extended-day component is closely linked to its during-school academic enrichment component—and the same team members staff both. Whereas other interventions are designed to promote either the students' learning or their development, ISA is a comprehensive intervention that focuses simultaneously on youth development and student learning. (Our research has demonstrated that ISA's 93% graduation rate could not have been predicted by either chance or comparison to other groups of U.S. students who had been identified as likely to drop out of school.)

Ben-Avie, Haynes, and Steinfeld administered our Learning and Development Inventory (LDI) to 261 ISA students from Long Island and Westchester County, New York.[3] The LDI is an outgrowth of 10 years of research at the Yale Child Study Center on the relationship between youth development and student learning. The high school version of LDI is a 95-item survey with a 5-point Likert response format that measures student learning and youth development. The middle school version of LDI is an abbreviated, 61-item scale. In 2002, the survey was administered to all middle and high schools in a Connecticut city. Data analysis was conducted on the responses to the survey to discern whether it met statisticians' criteria for being a reliable survey. This was found to be the case.[4]

The responses of the ISA students to the LDI were matched with those of a similar number of non-ISA students from around the country. The students were matched on the basis of enrollment in a low-performing school, low academic achievement, age, gender, socioeconomic status, and ethnic background, and/or exhibiting the following characteristics: failed one or more subjects and/or displayed transition problems, attendance problems, disciplinary problems, or family problems. The appendix to this chapter contains a description of the methodology that we used to provide a measure of cross-validation for our findings.

Our studies revealed several important predictors of students' academic perseverance (see Tables 1.2 and 1.3 in the appendix to this chapter), which we define as students' persistence in performing strategic behaviors that increase the likelihood of academic success, regardless of obstacles or distractions. In the order of their importance in our findings, these predictors were:

1. Students' ability to quickly recover their healthiest sense of self during and after challenging social situations (coping)
2. Students' feelings of efficacy when solving challenging problems in mathematics and science (problem solving in math and science)
3. Students' tendency to trust adults and to develop supportive relationships with them (engagement with adults)

These four themes of academic perseverance, coping, problem solving in math and science, and engagement with adults cluster throughout our findings in several major studies we have conducted.

What we learned is that as students' scores on the youth development dimension rose, so did their scores on the student learning dimension. The reverse was also true: Those students who tended to have low scores on the student learning dimension also tended to have low scores on the youth development dimension.[5]

We also learned how ISA staff members were able to shape the trajectory of the students' lifepaths—how, specifically, they were intervening. We already knew that to improve and increase cognitive engagement, ISA addressed the students' problem solving in math and science. To improve and increase behavioral engagement, ISA addressed the students' academic perseverance. To improve and increase psychological engagement, ISA addressed the students' coping skills and their engagement with adults. What we discovered when we went back to our research findings on ISA and other intervention programs was a driving force underlying all this effort: a belief system that promotes future orientation. These programs are founded on the belief that success is possible and that the way to achieve it is to insist on a graduated sequence of concrete skills that can support even somewhat abstract ideas about the long term. Thus, students who had been identified as most likely to drop out were now defying negative predictions about their future.

By seventh grade, we have found, students placed at risk of failure typically demonstrate that their orientation toward the future already diverges from the orientation of their more-likely-to-be-successful age mates. The orientation of students placed at risk of failure is marked by magical thinking ("Somehow, the project will get done in time"), by hoping for an external intermediary ("I'll win the lottery"), and/or by the expectation that the future will remain largely the same as the present ("I'll always live in a dangerous neighborhood"; "I wouldn't know how to behave in such a fancy office"). All these beliefs can support habits antithetical to academic excellence. In order for students to change, and in order for the adults who guide them to help them change, the students and adults must have and must demonstrate thoughts, feelings, and behaviors that support a positive attitude about the long-distant future and about themselves as successful learners and contributing members of society.

The relationship between potential future outcomes and present behavior for students is captured in the following passage by Lens and Moreas (1994):

> People with a long future time perspective . . . will experience less immediate satisfaction and more delayed satisfaction due to goal attainment (e.g., to become a nurse in two years vs. a medical doctor in seven years). However, the self-imposed delayed gratification that is inherent in long-term goal-setting cannot be reached by waiting. One usually has to perform a longer or shorter series of instrumental actions in order to achieve one's goals. (p. 27)

Strathman, Boninger, Gleicher, and Baker (1994) note the positive correlation found between future orientation and socioeconomic status. Students who experience pressing and, often, chronic traumatic immediate events (e.g., poverty and violence) tend not to take action to shape future outcomes. Yet ISA students showed that this does not need to be the case. The ISA staff members successfully inculcated in their formerly failing students the future orientation of successful students, and that future orientation and the self-identity that goes with it supported the students in their academic and personal growth. Whereas in students who have always been academically successful these attributes tend to predate school, it is clear that the attributes can be developed even after chronic school failure and can still promote school success. By their own self-report, in interview after interview, students chronicled their internal and external changes. The students' measurable academic success, accompanied by self-knowledge and ease at tracking their own reorientation from the past and into the far future, is an important part of what qualifies the entire ISA intervention as a series of positive developmental experiences.

WHERE TO START: A UNIVERSITY–SCHOOL DISTRICT PARTNERSHIP

In this section, we describe a partnership initiated by Drury University to impact students' developmental trajectories. We then describe a study that our Impact Analysis and Strategies Group conducted in partnership with Drury. We offer the partnership between Drury University and Springfield Public Schools in Missouri as an example: They did not address students' developmental needs by declaring that teachers will take care of promoting the students' learning and other school staff will take care of promoting the students' development. In this partnership, they adopted the approach of identifying the students' developmental needs and then using this knowledge to inform staff development activities for school staff members. Of special note, Drury offered a free master's degree to faculty in participating schools. As the partnership unfolded, Drury's school of education renamed itself the School of Education and Child Development.

In Springfield, Missouri, the Drury University School of Education and Child Development developed several partnerships that simultaneously promoted the learning and development of both preservice teachers and elementary, middle, and high school students. Preservice teachers had been coming to their professors asking for classroom management tips. One student suggested that the school of education "compile a book of recipes" to assist preservice teachers in dealing with a variety of classroom problems and issues. Jayne White, one of the authors of this chapter, realized that what teachers really need is an understanding of child and youth development. Armed with a deep understanding of their students, teachers should be able to prevent many classroom problems from occurring and should be able to foster the development of each student.

Although Drury's preservice teachers were exposed to developmental and learning theories in college, they did not yet understand the application of those theories to real situations, even though they had worked with children during each of their four field experiences. To discern how the professors were not adequately preparing the preservice teachers, the professors had many discussions with local educational leaders, parents, other teacher educators, and preservice teachers. The professors concluded that the preservice teachers were not spending enough time with any one child to make a difference. The preservice teachers would go to school X for a total of 15 hours and then go to school Y for a total of 15 hours. Never would they be in the same school two semesters in a row. They simply dropped in and dropped out. Mostly they were a nuisance to the teachers. Relationships were not established—although many hours were being expended. The reality was that neither party was really benefiting.

The professors at Drury decided that if they want preservice teachers to affect the lifepaths of children, then the preservice teachers must develop relationships with the children in their classrooms. This would require prolonged observation, interaction, and supervision in a school setting. There needed to be more structure and planning among the parties involved, and the college students needed to be assigned one or two children with whom they would work on a regular basis for a specified time (a semester or more). This would increase the possibility that relationships would form between youth and preservice teachers, thus increasing the likelihood that learning and development would be positively affected.

The First Phases of the Partnership

In the face of the district's desire to close Boyd/Berry, an elementary school located one block from the university and serving as a field experience site for preservice teachers, Drury proposed forming a partnership with the school. This partnership became guided by the Yale Child Study Center's School Development Program in 1997.

In 1996, Boyd/Berry was the lowest-performing school in the district, with the highest attrition rate of teachers, the highest mobility rate of students, the lowest levels of parent involvement, the greatest number of discipline problems, the highest rate of absenteeism, and the highest rate of suspensions. Since then, improvements have occurred in every area, including student achievement in math. Second-grade math scores on the Missouri Mastery and Achievement Tests increased from 250 in 1995–96 to 307 in 1999–2000. Third-grade math scores increased during this period from 290 to 334. Fifth-grade math scores increased from 280 to 349. In Missouri, student performance on standardized tests (Missouri Assessment Project) is categorized. In 2000, 27% of Boyd/Berry students achieved in the advanced and proficient category, an increase from 4.5% one year before (statewide, 38% of students performed in this category).

The partnership was expanded into Pipkin Middle School, the usual middle school of students from Boyd/Berry. At the same time, the coordinator of Drury's Student Services received funding from the Community Partnership of the Ozarks to implement an initiative known as TASK (Taking a Stand for Kids). TASK provides many opportunities for Drury students to become involved in service-oriented experiences. As a group, Drury's TASK preservice teacher students contribute about 2,000 hours a year of direct involvement with students, parents, and faculty through: (1) tutoring and mentoring at Central High School (CHS), Pipkin Middle School, and Boyd/Berry Elementary School during the school day; tutoring and mentoring after school at the Boys and Girls Club of Springfield, and Big Brothers/Big Sisters of Springfield; (2) volunteering at the Missouri Hotel, a shelter for homeless families; (3) working with children enrolled in the Head Start Program; and (4) volunteering to work with women and children at the Family Violence Center. Drury's professors have begun teaching courses to the preservice teachers on the premises at Boyd/Berry and Pipkin.

CHS Joins the Partnership

During the 2000–01 school year, CHS engaged in planning to become a partner. CHS faculty agreed to collaborate more closely with Drury to accept preservice teachers for methods courses, practicums, and other field experiences (including student teaching). CHS also agreed to send faculty to the School Development Program national leadership academies. In return, Drury offered CHS faculty tuition remission for graduate study, and provided mentoring and other opportunities for CHS students. (Forty faculty members from the three partnership schools enrolled in a total of more than 360 credit hours of graduate coursework during the 2000–01 academic year.)

The data contained in this section are baseline data for CHS. Most of the 1,139 students at CHS are White (approximately 80%). The next largest group is African American (approximately 10%), and there are small minorities of Hispanics, Asians, and Native Americans in the school. Forty-one percent of the students receive free or reduced-price lunch, a poverty indicator. The school has a 56% mobility factor, compared with 35%, 32%, 17%, and 13% in Springfield's four other high schools. The Springfield Public Schools' Annual Report indicates a 1999 graduation rate of 43%. This improved to 52% for the class of 2000.

As part of CHS's planning year (the year prior to actual implementation of the SDP) to help decide where to focus interventions, the Learning and Development Inventory, which had been slightly revised in 2001, was administered. Our findings from its administration to 700 students at CHS once again confirm our findings about the relationship between learning and development. We observed that the relationship between the learning dimension and the development dimension was strong.[6] The slightly revised variables were also found to be sound. These include the new future orientation variable, academic persistence (formerly academic perseverance), problem solving in math (formerly problem solving in math and science), and seeking adult guidance (formerly engagement with adults).

We also found that the most important predictors of academic and professional competencies were future orientation, academic persistence, and coping. Academic and professional competencies is the variable that measures the consistent demonstration of attributes, such as work ethic, that contribute to high academic achievement and that employers consider desirable in new employees. Relationships between future orientation and several other variables were consistent with what we expected based on experience and prior research. (The statistics that support these statements appear in the statistical tables at the end of the appendix to this chapter.) The following variables also were found to be correlated with problem solving in math: academic and professional competencies,[7] academic persistence,[8] student engagement,[9] academic focus,[10] and language skills.[11] The relationship between future orientation and problem solving in math was observed to be statistically significant.[12] In the following section, we focus on future orientation, the ability to conceive of one's own development.

FUTURE ORIENTATION: THE MOST IMPORTANT PREDICTOR OF ACADEMIC AND PROFESSIONAL COMPETENCIES

The CHS students were asked to indicate their immediate plans for formal education after high school. A data analysis was conducted to see whether significant differences could be discerned between those planning to attend a 4-year college and those not planning to do so. On every single student learning and youth development variable, those planning to attend a 4-year college had significantly higher scores than those not planning to attend a 4-year college.

CHS teachers commented at a panel discussion and in subsequent discussions that there appears to be a discrepancy between students' self-reports on plans to attend 4-year colleges and the teachers' observations of patterns of student behavior. Consistent with the results of previous studies that we conducted on students' temporal orientation, students who had higher future orientation scores tended to indicate more often that they planned to attend 4-year colleges. This was particularly the case with students who would not be the first in their families to attend college. Moreover, students who had visited a college campus tended to have higher scores on future orientation. The comments from CHS teachers, however, suggested that many students had no serious plans for continuing their education after high school, as evidenced by their not having taken the steps to apply for college enrollment (e.g., taking the ACT test, completing financial aid forms, and visiting college campuses). Based on these comments, we conducted further analyses to generate possible explanations for this discrepancy.

Present and future orientations tend to be important influences on a person's behavior, and the two are not necessarily opposites of each other (i.e., a person can be both highly future- and present-oriented). We found that students who indicated that they planned to attend a 4-year college and who had family members who attended college were not only more future-oriented but also less present-oriented than their peers who had other educational plans or who would be the first in their family to attend college. These results possibly explain the magical thinking that we have observed in other student populations: Students do have future aspirations for attending college but are engaged or preoccupied with present activities. One teacher stated, "It does not appear to be a byproduct of hopelessness; rather it seems to flow from an attitude of *carpe diem*. They seem to focus on living and cruising through each day to the point that thinking about or planning what they will do tomorrow or in 4 years is ridiculous."

It is possible, indeed likely, that some students said that they planned to attend a 4-year college because of convention or wanting to look good on their survey. Regardless of the reason, they expressed aspirations for the future that included college, and the gap between their future plans and present behaviors represents an important opportunity for intervention. James P. Comer has taught us that the quality of relationships impacts students' level of future orientation. Therefore, we conducted a further analysis using items from the survey that measure students' social relationships with other students and items that measure student–teacher relationships. We found that students who had high-quality relationships with both peers and teachers tended to have the highest levels of future orientation. This finding supports the premise that the adults at CHS can influence their students' future orientation and enhance their educational outcomes.

ENHANCING SUCCESS IN THE CHARACTERISTICS THAT CORRELATE WITH PROBLEM SOLVING IN MATH AND SCIENCE

During school hours, students provide us with a glimpse of who they are. Taking a youth development perspective means widening our view of students to include the student as a member of a family and community (hence the need for school/community/university partnerships). Moreover, an understanding of youth development enables us to see the student as an individual in the process of becoming—as an individual moving along a lifepath. Succeeding in math is not only about understanding math, it is about the whole trajectory of a child's life. Today algebra is a youth development issue. Because literacy in math and science opens the gateway to college and life success, the lifepaths of today's students will be influenced by whether or not they can excel in their math and science classes.

The baseline data from CHS show that, in general, students' time orientation is focused on the present, not on the future. Students will not buy the educational utility argument (i.e., if you study hard now, it will pay off in the future). In this case, raising standards is probably the least effective solution. J. P. Comer (personal communication, 1997) told us, "You can't challenge students if they are not willing to perform. You can challenge them and some will reach the standards—those that have a sense of well-being, a sense of hope, a belief that there is opportunity in their future—those that have been prepared and disciplined by a caring home experience, and by a caring community experience."

We have found that ensuring that students are supported in their development is too important an issue to leave to add-on programs or to the initiative of the teacher working in isolation. Algebra must be integral to the school day, and so must youth development. School communities that promote students' developmental experiences are those that simultaneously address students' development and learning. Adding programs that address only one dimension or the other—or only some aspects of youth development—will only crowd an already overcrowded curriculum. Our experience has shown us the benefits of implementing a process of balancing the curriculum. Balancing the curriculum requires a partnership on the scale of the Drury University partnership.

CONCLUSION

Helping students to multiply their options and decreasing the number of students who float through the school day are youth development topics that go far beyond introducing a developmentally appropriate curriculum, raising standards, or establishing accountability measures. Creative mathematical and scientific thinking relies on the ability to create flexible internal images. Flexible thinking is more likely in children who have been exposed to many kinds of experiences, who have been encouraged to see the world metaphorically as well as concretely, who have access to their inner visions, and who have the linguistic skills to share them. When youth are developing well, they learn well.

POSTSCRIPT

In 1999, when the Third International Mathematics and Science Study—Repeat (TIMSS-R) was administered, Guilford County Schools had used our School Development Program to merge three very different school systems (see Comer, Ben-Avie, Haynes, & Joyner, 1999) and had piloted our balanced curriculum process. The TIMSS-R results showed that their gamble had paid off: Guilford County students excelled in math and science, scoring 27 points above the international average in mathematics and 46 points higher than the international average in science. Guilford County eighth graders scored 12 points above the U.S. average in mathematics and 19 points above the U.S. average in science (Guilford County Schools, 2001). This finding is all the more thought-provoking when one considers socioeconomic factors: According to the school system's website, "The 1999 data reveal that 37 percent of Guilford County Schools' participants were from families who are eligible to receive free or reduced-price meals, classifying them as low-income. The top scoring U.S. systems had only 2–14 percent of their participants from low-income families" (Guilford County Schools, 2001).

APPENDIX: RESEARCH DESIGN AND RESULTS

The direction that our research has taken rests on previous studies that we conducted over a 10-year period at the Yale Child Study Center. The following are brief descriptions of three of these foundational studies:

- In 1995, we administered the *Behavior Assessment Schedule for Students* (Haynes, 1995) to a total of 831 students in School Development Program schools. BASS is designed to measure students' self-reported thinking and beliefs about their social interactions and problems. We also retrieved the students' achievement scores in mathematics. The relationship between students' social knowledge of themselves and others and their achievement in mathematics was found to be very strong.[13]
- We conducted a study that was designed to examine the use of specific learning and cognitive strategies as well as students' achievement motivation. Seventy-two female and 76 male tenth-grade students who attended a School Development Program urban high school in the northeastern United States participated in the study. We obtained the students' quality point averages (QPAs), which are derived from a grading system based on weighted scores for higher-track courses. The students completed the *Learning and Study Strategy Inventory* (LASSI; Weinstein, Zimmerman, & Palmer, 1988). The LASSI looks at students' methodologies for learning and processing information. The results of the study indicated that cognitive and motivational factors are significantly related to student learning and achievement.[14] Motivation was the strongest variable in predicting a student's QPA.[15] The next-strongest predictor was the information processing variable. Average and high-achieving students

did not significantly differ on any of the LASSI subscales. Low-achieving students, however, differed significantly from average and high-achieving students on every single LASSI subscale. We understand from the LASSI study that the action steps of math and science are the rigorous methodologies that enable us to organize information under the rubric of scientific concepts, filter out irrelevant information, analyze facts critically, share interpretations of findings with colleagues, and engage in problem solving. And these methodologies can be learned.

- In our research on academic self-concept among 146 middle school students, we found the climate of relationships within classrooms—between teachers and students as well as among students—to be significantly related to the intellectual and school-status dimension of self-concept.[16] This dimension reflects children's self-assessments of their abilities with respect to intellectual and academic tasks (see Piers, 1986). Improvements in the climate of classroom relationships may indirectly affect student achievement in math and science. For example, Emmons, Haynes, Owen, Bility, and Comer (1994) present research that shows that self-concept is a mediator of student achievement. A systematic pattern of relationships among self-concept, classroom climate, behavior, and achievement was observed. Specifically, three significant paths were found: one from classroom climate to self-concept,[17] one from self-concept to behavior,[18] and one from behavior to achievement.[19]

Definition of Survey Variables

In this chapter, we discuss youth development and student learning in terms of competencies. Table 1.1 shows the definitions of the variables that we measure in our surveys.

Methodology

We used a triangulated approach that provided a measure of cross-validation of the findings:

1. To determine the extent to which positive trends may be discerned with regard to student outcomes, we conducted a retroactive analysis on the achievement data of the first four ISA cohorts (167 students) and a cohort analysis of the ISA class of 2000 from four schools.
2. To determine the quality of program implementation at the sites, we (1) conducted 70 direct observations of regularly scheduled ISA academic enrichment and counseling class periods, and (2) adminis-

Table 1.1. Definitions of Variables

Learning and Development Inventory (LDI)	Definition
Learning subscale	
Demographic questions	Items exploring the respondent's gender, age, mobility, plans for formal education after high school, and out-of-school time
Academic and professional competencies	The consistent demonstration of attributes (e.g., work ethic) that contribute to high academic achievement and that employers consider desirable in new employees
Academic focus	Student's tendency to focus attention on academic work, especially with respect to keeping schoolwork organized
Academic persistence	Student's persistence in performing strategic behaviors that increase the likelihood of academic success, regardless of obstacles or distractions
Student engagement	Student's engagement with schooling and motivation for high academic achievement
Language skills	Degree to which student feels comfortable and effective using language in both academic and interpersonal settings
Problem solving in math	Student's feelings of efficacy when solving challenging problems in mathematics
Development subscale	
Coping	The ability to quickly recover one's healthiest sense of self during and after challenging social situations
Belonging	Feelings of connection and affiliation with the student body at the school or others in the respondent's general age group
Future orientation	The ability to conceive of one's own development—the tendency to devote attention to the future, set goals beyond the immediate time frame, and engage in behaviors designed to reach future goals
Friendship	Perceptions of intimacy with particular persons and participation in close friendships with other students
Seeking adult guidance	The tendency to seek out adults for guidance and to develop supportive relationships with them
Safety	Items exploring the respondent's sense of safety at school and on the way to and from school
Demographic questions	Items exploring the respondent's participation in extracurricular activities, ethnicity, grade point average, and other background information

tered our Staff Feedback Form to 73 ISA school-based staff members.

3. Our direct observations of ISA enrichment and counseling sessions and analysis of the assessments of the ISA faculty regarding their effectiveness helped us to interpret the students' responses to the Learning and Development Inventory.

We also conducted interviews with ISA staff members at all levels and with students throughout the 3 years of the study.

Statistical Tables

Table 1.2. Major Predictors of Academic Perseverance

Variable	R	R^2	Adjusted R^2	Beta
Coping	.569	.324	.318	.569[**]
Math/science	.674	.454	.444	.389[**]
Adults	.693	.481	.466	.190[*]

[*]$p < .05.$ [**]$p < .0001.$

Table 1.3. Major Predictors of Academic and Professional Competencies

Variable	R^2	Adjusted R^2	Beta
Future orientation	.390	.389	.354[*]
Academic persistence	.481	.480	.299[*]
Coping	.524	.522	.237[*]

[*]$p < .001$

NOTES

1. IASG members who are authors of this chapter are Ben-Avie, Haynes, and Steinfeld.

2. $r = .80$, $p = .04$.

3. Students from the following school districts: Roosevelt Union Free School District, Long Island; Wyandanch Union Free School District, Long Island; Enlarged City of Troy Public Schools, New York State Capitol Region; Hempstead Union Free School District, Long Island; and City of Mount Vernon Public Schools, Westchester County.

4. The internal consistency reliability for LDI was found to be in the robust high range (.947).

5. $r = .764$, $p < .001$.

6. $r = .650$, $p = .001$.

7. $r = .293$, $p = .001$.

8. $r = .310$, $p = .001$.

9. $r = .357$, $p = .001$.

10. $r = .368$, $p = .001$.

11. $r = .391$, $p = .001$.

12. $r = .282$, $p < .001$.

13. For the eighth-grade students, the strength of the relationship was found to be .80 ($p = .04$).

14. $F(20,268) = 2.6$, $p < .0001$.

15. $R = .45$, $F(1,146) = 37.8$, $p < .0001$, accounting for 21% ($R^2 = .205$) of the observed variance in QPA.

16. $r = .43$, $p < .01$.

17. .62.

18. .78.

19. .47.

REFERENCES

Anderson, J. (1981). *Thinking, changing, rearranging: Improving self-esteem in young people.* Portland, OR: Metamorphous Press.

Bredo, E. (1997). The social construction of learning. In G. Phye (Ed.), *Handbook of academic learning: The construction of knowledge* (pp. 3–45). San Diego: Academic Press.

Bruner, J. S. (1977). *The process of education.* Cambridge, MA: Harvard University Press.

Comer, J. P., Ben-Avie, M., Haynes, N. M., & Joyner, E. T. (1999). *Child by child: The Comer process for change in education.* New York: Teachers College Press.

Dewey, J. (1938). *Experience and education.* New York: Collier Books.

Dilts, R. B. (1998). *Modeling with NLP.* Capitola, CA: Meta.

Dilts, R. B. (1999). *Sleight of mouth: The magic of conversational belief change.* Capitola, CA: Meta.

Emmons, C. L., Haynes, N. M., Owen, S. V., Bility, K., & Comer, J. P. (1994). Self-concept as a mediator of school climate effects. In N. M. Haynes, *School Development Program Research Monograph* (pp. 1–41). New Haven: Yale Child Study Center.

Fischler, M. S. (1998, April 5). Giving schoolchildren tools to succeed. *New York Times,* p. 25.

Guilford County Schools (2001). www.guilford.k12.nc.us/news/tims_start.htm

Haynes, N. M. (1995). *Behavior Assessment Schedule for Students.* New Haven, CT: Yale Child Study Center.

Lens, W., & Moreas, M. (1994). Future time perspective: Individual and societal approach. In Z. Zaleski (Ed.), *Psychology of future orientation* (pp. 23–38). Lublin, Poland: Scientific Society of the Catholic University of Lublin.

O'Connor, J., & Seymour, J. (1990). *Introducing neuro-linguistic programming.* Cornwall, U.K.: Aquarian Press.

Piers, E. V. (1986). *The Piers-Harris Children's Self-Concept Scale: Revised manual.* Los Angeles: Western Psychological Service.

Strathman, A., Boninger, D., Gleicher, F., & Baker, S. (1994). Constructing the future with present behavior: An individual difference approach. In Z. Zaleski (Ed.), *Psychology of future orientation* (pp. 107–120). Lublin, Poland: Scientific Society of the Catholic University of Lublin.

Vygotsky, L. S. (1978). *Mind in society.* Cambridge, MA: Harvard University Press.

Weinstein, C. E., Zimmerman, S. A., & Palmer, D. R. (1988). Assessing learning strategies: The design and development of the LASSI. In C. E. Weinstein, E. T. Goetz, & P. A. Alexander (Eds.), *Learning and study strategies: Issues in assessment, instruction, and evaluation* (pp. 25–40). San Diego: Academic Press.

ADDITIONAL READINGS

Haynes, N. M., & Emmons, C. L. (1997). *A summary of SDP effects: A ten year review.* New Haven: Yale Child Study Center.

U.S. Department of Education. (1997). *Mathematics equals opportunity.* White paper prepared for U.S. Secretary of Education Richard W. Riley.

Vygotsky, L. S. (1992). *Thought and language.* Cambridge, MA: MIT Press.

Vygotsky, L. S. (1994). The problem of the environment. In R. Van Der Veer & J. Valsiner (Eds.), *The Vygotsky reader* (pp. 338–355). Oxford, UK: Blackwell.

CHAPTER 2

Connecting with Students on a Social and Emotional Level Through In-Depth Discussions of Mathematics

John S. Zeuli & Michael Ben-Avie

MATHEMATICS AND SCIENCE TEACHERS have been encouraged to gear their lessons to students' ability to reason and to students' social and emotional development. Yet, given the diverse needs of their students, many teachers find it difficult to make the lessons relevant in this way while remaining true to math concepts. In this chapter, we offer insights into how teachers can use in-depth discussions of mathematics to deliver high-quality lessons while supporting their students' social and emotional development as individual learners and as members of a community of learners.

We examine the classroom teaching of teachers who were attempting to tie mathematics to the larger arena of experience—often called "the real world"—of which a student's school life is only one part. Our comments are based on a study that included observations and interviews of 25 elementary and middle school teachers of mathematics whose responses to the Third International Mathematics and Science Study (TIMSS) suggested that what and how they taught approximated reformers' recommendations. These teachers described themselves as familiar with national and state reform documents in mathematics. They considered it important that "students understand how mathematics is used in the real world," and many stated that they encouraged students to reason in their mathematics lessons.

The teachers we describe in this chapter emphasize concept-oriented mathematical knowledge. Steering clear of narrow utilitarian or traditional views of education (in which students learn basic skills for practical use or acquire information by rote), reformers recommend that teachers engage students in thinking about the world outside school using conceptual frameworks drawn from the discipline of mathematics. We are keenly interested in concept formation because it is essential for reflective thinking by individuals and groups. Too often, students have only a verbal label for a concept (i.e., they know only the concept's name). To truly form concepts, however, one must also learn their meaning, how to apply them to new situations, and how to participate in the ways of life of reflective thinkers and/or professional networks. These are major concerns for youth developers. Every time a teacher helps a student truly learn a concept in this multifaceted way, the learning not only enhances the student's appreciation of the subject matter but also strengthens the student's ability to function successfully as a creative, thoughtful, and communicative member of society.

In the closing section of the chapter, we discuss implications for implementing new wide-scale reforms in math and science.

MAKING MATHEMATICS RELEVANT

Making mathematics relevant to students figures prominently in recent reform documents articulating a new vision of teaching and learning mathematics (e.g., National Council of Teachers of Mathematics [NCTM], 1989, 1991; see also American Association for the Advancement of Science [AAAS], 1993; National Research Council, 1996). The NCTM *Curriculum and Evaluation Standards* (1989) recommends that teachers in the K–4 curriculum connect mathematics to students' everyday experiences both in and outside school, and recommends that in grades 5–8 students perceive and value the role of mathematics in our culture and society. AAAS's *Science for All Americans* (Rutherford & Ahlgren, 1990) also emphasizes the importance of students recognizing the real-world significance of mathematics as well as science, highlighting the wide range of useful applications from both of these disciplines. While connections to the real world are not the sole or primary focus in these reform documents, these connections often signify a starting point and a context for facilitating students' understanding of fundamental mathematical ideas and applications.

In a 5-year study, however, we found that many of the teachers who introduced real-world problems and connected mathematics to students' daily lives were not implementing the new vision of mathematics education. The great majority of teachers were still guiding students toward "the officially sanctioned solution method" (see Cobb, Wood, & Yackel, 1993) or emphasizing a narrow utilitarianism in the form of practical skills. The mathematical knowledge in these teachers' classrooms was procedural, and "doing" mathematics was still interpreted as getting the answer right. The kind of conjecturing, reasoning, and defending of mathematical ideas and solution strategies that reformers encourage were either not prominent or notably absent from these teachers' classrooms. It was not, however, that the majority of teachers had failed to alter their teaching over the past several years in the direction of the reforms. We found that they included new mathematical problems in their curriculum, made extensive use of manipulatives, and altered classroom grouping patterns. The problem was that the majority had not yet altered what they taught as the nature of mathematical knowledge or what it meant to do mathematics.

Several teachers in our study, however, had a different set of assumptions about mathematical knowledge and how students might acquire it. The mathematical knowledge in their classrooms was principled, that is, it involved mathematical concepts that students could use to construct strategies or procedures to solve problems (Lampert, 1986). And doing mathematics meant attempting to explain one's mathematical reasoning and devising and defending solutions to problems (Ball, 1992, 1993; Cobb et al., 1993; Lampert, 1990, 1992; Simon, 1986). We call teachers whose teaching reflected this view of what it means to know and do mathematics concept-oriented. Although a minority in this study, the concept-oriented teachers in fact had made mathematics relevant to students in the ways that reformers envision. Doing mathematics in their classrooms meant that students made conjectures, provided evidence, and sought mathematical explanations to problems that teachers tied to the world outside school.

That relatively few teachers' classroom teaching would approximate the central intent of the reforms should not be surprising. Even though the NCTM Standards (1989, 1991) have been out for over a decade, learning to teach in ways that recognize and support new conceptions of knowledge, learning, and teaching is no straightforward, simple task. Most of the teachers in our sample whose mathematics teaching approximated the reforms had been participants in extended professional development devoted to transforming what teachers taught and how they taught mathematics (Spillane & Zeuli, 1997; Thompson & Zeuli, 1999). Because this kind of transformative professional development is relatively rare within states and districts, one might expect the reforms to progress slowly and a bit erratically, even among teachers who obviously accept many reform ideas and are making attempts to alter their teaching in light of them.

HOW WE SELECTED THE TEACHERS FOR THE STUDY

The research reported here is part of a 5-year multiphase study that examined the educational policy system and mathematics and science teaching in the state of Michigan. The early phases of the project focused on local educational authorities' instructional policy making in nine school districts that differed in location, size, and composition. The later phases examined the effects of state and local policy making on the mathematics and science teaching of teachers in these districts (see Spillane & Thompson, 1997; Spillane & Zeuli, 1997; Thompson, Zeuli, & Borman, 1997). Participating teachers were selected on the basis of their responses to a subset of items on the TIMSS Population 1 (third and fourth grade) and Population 2 (seventh and eighth grade) questionnaires. The TIMSS questionnaires were not designed to measure progress toward implementing mathematics and science reforms in the United States. However, we were able to identify a set of items that were closely related to reform ideas, such as how often a teacher asks students to explain the reasoning behind a mathematical idea or how often a teacher provides students with problems for which there is no immediate and obvious method of solution. Based on items such as these, we were able to construct a scale of reform practices in mathematics, science, and a combination of the two.

Teachers who were selected for observations and interviews had scored near the top among nearly 400 respondents on the subset of items related to the reforms in mathematics and science. Of the 25 teachers selected for further study, 18 were elementary mathematics teachers and seven were middle school mathematics teachers. Six of the teachers in the study taught middle school science, and there was one elementary teacher who taught only science. Teachers included in the study were distributed across district types and locations within the state. This chapter discusses the teachers who most closely approximated the reformers' ideals.

The teachers were observed and interviewed twice—with the exception of one elementary teacher who was observed only once due to scheduling difficulties. During classroom observations, researchers took careful notes and frequently audiotaped large portions of each lesson to capture whole-class and small-group discussions. Each lesson observed was reported on in a lesson narrative of 5–15 single-spaced pages. All interviews were transcribed. The reports of the observed lessons and the transcribed interviews were then coded by categories. The coding categories for the mathematics lessons corresponded to the main features of the content and pedagogy standards as reflected in the NCTM Standards (1989, 1991), described in the next section. Teachers' lessons and interviews also were coded, using the categories "all students" (whether the teachers responded to all the students in the classroom) and "influences" (teachers' accounts of the factors that shaped changes in their mathematics teaching, for example, state tests and curriculum guides or various kinds of professional development). The findings of the study, as well as the vignettes presented later indicating what and how teachers taught, are derived from these analytic memoranda.

WAYS TO MAKE MATHEMATICS RELEVANT

Contemporary reform documents (NCTM, 1989, 1991) argue for a vision of mathematical knowledge that is chiefly conceptual and involves four key components—mathematics as problem solving, mathematics as communication, mathematics as reasoning, and mathematical connections. Real-world relevance is emphasized in two of the content standards: mathematical problem solving and mathematical connections.

Problem solving should be at the center of the mathematics curriculum. Problem solving should both permeate the entire mathematics program and provide a context for students to learn mathematical concepts and skills. Problem solving is not a topic on which students focus separately from the remainder of the curriculum, nor should it be simply a context in which students practice basic skills or apply already learned procedures or formulas. Problems should be open-ended and require logical reasoning. In order to solve problems, students should have to explore and find patterns. NCTM emphasizes further that students must learn a variety of ways to represent problems as well as strategies to solve them. Specifically, NCTM (1989, pp. 23–25, 75–78) argues that students should learn to use problem-solving approaches to (1) investigate and understand mathematics, (2) formulate problems that arise from everyday, real-world contexts as well as from strictly mathematical contexts, (3) develop and apply strategies to solve a variety of problems and to explore mathematical ideas, (4) verify and interpret results with respect to the original problem, (5) generalize solutions and strategies to new problem situations (grades 5–8), and (6) gain confidence in using mathematics meaningfully.

Mathematics as communication is also key. Mathematics can be viewed as a language, as a way of talking about and representing ideas. Communication involves giving students opportunities to talk mathematics so that they construct new understandings of mathematical concepts and appreciate different ways of representing mathematical ideas (symbolic, physical, verbal, pictorial, and mental representations). This kind of talking helps students to develop links between their informal, intuitive notions and the abstract and symbolic language of mathematics. It also helps them develop three important habits: (1) the habit of describing something going on in their heads clearly enough so that another person can accurately grasp their meaning, (2) the habit of being okay while being observed during these descriptions, and (3) the habit of helping others be okay while being observed during these descriptions. Whether what they are describing is their solution or their confusion, the ability to think and speak while being the center of attention is an essential element of both successful schooling and successful life outside school. The teacher, therefore, is the crucial model of respectful listener, questioner, and supporter while students in the process of solving a problem grope for clarity. The teacher must demonstrate consistently that acceptance as a member of the class is not simply a function of being quick to get the right answer.

It is worthwhile to pause for a moment to talk about the type of social context that supports students' thinking through and evaluating mathematical ideas and procedures. One of the unintended consequences of teaching toward the officially sanctioned solution method is that students and teachers become uncomfortable with not knowing. They squelch their natural curiosity to discover how to think about the problem, and they become—sometimes unconsciously—anxious until they produce the right answer. Most students have a perception about who is getting the right answer—and who is not. Their attention is divided; only part of it is on the content area, and the rest—sometimes the lion's share—is on expectations of success and failure and their rank in the social and intellectual hierarchy of the class. And with these expectations there is often a bad feeling that works against new learning. There is a difference between feeling good and feeling socially and emotionally competent. Feeling socially and emotionally competent is a prerequisite for sustaining the desire to learn. Students and teachers should be reinforced in their ability to feel socially and emotionally competent even when they don't know "the" answer and also while learning how to learn and remember.

Reasoning and justifying solutions and processes are pivotal. Rather than merely memorizing mathematics facts and procedures, students make conjectures, offer evidence, and attempt to build an argument in support of their mathematical thinking. As students make sense of mathematics, they draw on and create models, or cite other mathematical facts or relationships as ways to justify their thinking. Because mathematics is reasoning, the focus is on how students think in response to a problem, not simply whether they obtain the right answer.

NCTM further underscores the importance of students making a variety of mathematical connections, including connections between mathematics and their own daily lives (NCTM, 1989, pp. 32–35, 84–86). Reformers emphasize other connections, such as helping students understand the relationship between mathematical concepts and procedures, how big mathematical ideas are linked across different mathematical topics, integrating mathematical ideas with other subject areas, and connecting various representations of concepts or procedures to one another. These kinds of mathematical connections are important if students are to perceive mathematics as an integrated whole and not simply an academic exercise with no bearing on what they see and do in the world around them.

Of course, making these sorts of fundamental changes in what counts as mathematical knowledge and what it means to do mathematics in classrooms depends on teachers changing their pedagogy (Ball, 1992; Lampert, 1986, 1990). That is, the tasks (questions, problems, and exercises) students work on should involve significant mathematical concepts and ideas that students can use to devise and test procedures to solve problems. The tasks should present mathematics as a process of reasoning and problem solving and not a process of following the teacher's guidance to calculate a right answer or the application of previously memorized or readily acquired formulas or procedures. Classroom discourse patterns (the ways the teacher and students talk, think, agree, and disagree) should reflect the direction of the tasks. The teacher should ask questions that seek to discover students' mathematical thinking; students are expected to talk, model, and explain their ideas using a range of symbols and concrete materials. This is accomplished within a collaborative environment (the interplay of the physical, social, and intellectual context) where the teacher and students are engaged in a joint effort to understand and use mathematical ideas. Teachers also must continually analyze or assess the tasks, discourse, and learning environment in an effort to understand the extent to which they are promoting mathematical power in each student.

The Standards call special attention to tasks that engage students in open-ended, real-world problems that pervade the curriculum and require disciplined exploration and logical reasoning to solve. But reformers do not suggest that problems must be drawn from real life. They may be drawn from mathematical content as long as they remain open-ended and make possible the sort of sense making and reasoning that reformers encourage. As Hiebert and colleagues (1996) show, students may find meaning and relevance in problems drawn solely from the domain of mathematics. Connecting students' mathematical thinking to their daily lives or outside experience may occur after students have worked exclusively within the domain of mathematics.

Perspective on the connections of real life to disciplinary learning is the subject of long-standing debates in the philosophy of education and the psychology of learning. Both Dewey and Vygotsky, for example, were interested in how schooling, specifically instruction, could facilitate students' cognitive development. But they differed on the starting point of the curriculum, with danger attendant on each side. If, as Dewey (1902/1956, 1933, 1938/1963) suggests, the students' everyday world serves as a starting point for inquiry, the danger is that students never achieve any conceptual elevation from familiar terrain (see Floden & Buchmann, 1993). If, as Vygotsky (1962) suggests, the curriculum initially focuses on students exploring conceptual relationships within a discipline apart from everyday experience, the danger is that students perceive disciplinary knowledge as remote and arbitrary (see Davydov, 1975; Martin, 1990). Both perspectives state outright or imply that the teacher's role is critical. Vygotsky (1978) emphasized teachers' scaffolding within students' zone of proximal development, and Dewey (1904/1965) characterized the teacher as responsible for engaging students in meaningful activity and monitoring student thinking. Still, subsequent connections to the real world must be accomplished within a social context that supports students' thinking through and evaluating mathematical ideas and procedures.

In addition to taking something salient in the students' environment and using that as the content of a math problem, schools could impact students' development through taking something that is not currently salient in their environment and making it salient. Making mathematics relevant does not mean limiting oneself to only what currently exists within the students' lives. For many students, their world is limited to about four square blocks. A tension exists between providing students with access to the broader real life and respecting their current real life. The ideal is to be both respectful of the students' current real life and enthusiastic about presenting them with an even larger arena in which to really live.

All teachers in our subsample reported teaching in ways consistent with reformers' recommendations (e.g., use of concrete materials and small-group work), and all teachers considered it important to make mathematics meaningful to students. Commonalities also existed among teachers in how the real world entered their classrooms, whether they introduced a real-world problem or in some other way attempted to connect mathematics to students' everyday lives. Several teachers, for example, asked students to devise mathematical story problems. On the surface, teachers' approaches had the potential to promote reformers' visions of real-life mathematics, although few teachers actually did so.

In the following sections, we describe and illustrate the approaches of teachers whose mathematics teaching reflected differences in how they implemented real-world relevance in their classrooms.

EMPHASIZING CONCEPT-ORIENTED MATHEMATICAL KNOWLEDGE

Four of our surveyed 25 teachers taught concept-oriented lessons. They emphasized mathematical ideas and concepts that students could use to construct strategies or procedures to solve problems. The manner in which the real world entered their classrooms differed, as did aspects of the pedagogy through which students attempted to reason about mathematical ideas. One reform-oriented, middle school teacher, Ms. Howard (pseudonym) included mathematical tasks reflecting real-world problems. A few days before we observed her first lesson, Howard had begun a unit on extrapolation. On the overhead was placed a rectangular figure that contained hundreds of tiny dots. Students were asked to imagine that the rectangle was a field and the dots were people standing in the field. Before introducing the idea of sampling, Howard briefly reviewed the various strategies students had devised to determine the estimated population:

> You figured out different ways to determine how many people are in the whole field. Some students counted each and every person, other students drew a grid and counted people within the grid and then tried to generalize to the broader population. A few of you tried to

count the dots in the area, while others tried to figure out the pattern of dots, estimate the pattern for a particular section, and then see how many sections in the total area. When you use a grid to figure the number of dots, you were drawing a sample.

Howard then asked students a question that would occupy their efforts over the next several days: "We are going to look at what biologists do to figure out the wildlife population in a particular area. What do they do to count wildlife?" Students generated some hypotheses (e.g., they count how many deer cross the Mackinaw Bridge; they bait them). After piquing the students' curiosity, Howard did not pursue their ideas at that juncture, but placed students in groups of four and explained a simulation students would do. She had 32-ounce glass jars filled with—in all—tens of hundreds of white jellybeans.

The forest will be the glass jar, and the deer will be the jellybeans. I am going to take from the glass jar (the forest) 100 jellybeans (deer) and then replace (tag) the original jellybeans with 100 gold jellybeans. We are then going to mix the 100 gold jellybeans back into the beans in the jar and then pull out samples of beans. Get into groups of four and draw samples. First take out 1 scoop of beans and count how many gold beans are in the sample and how many regular jellybeans. Then mix the first scoop back into the jar and pull out 2 scoops of beans. Count the number of gold beans in the scoops and the regular beans. Mark it down. Put the scoops back into the jar and do the same thing for 3, 4, and 5 scoops of jellybeans. Remember to mix well the 100 gold jellybeans into the regular beans before you start getting scoops.

Students had difficulty determining what tagging was and how it was connected to the overall problem. Eventually all the groups drew samples of jellybeans from the glass jars and noted on poster paper the number of gold (tagged) and white (regular) jellybeans they had scooped out. Below is an example of what one group placed on the chalkboard for classmates to examine.

Group 1	# of gold beans in scoop	# of regular beans
sample 1 (1 scoop)	3	49
sample 2 (2 scoops)	4	78
sample 3 (3 scoops)	3	137
sample 4 (4 scoops)	7	177
sample 5 (5 scoops)	16	208

Students were asked to "study the sample data and figure out the total number of beans in the glass jar." Students, once again, generated a series of hypotheses:

> It's kinda like how we did the population grid.

> We have to find a way to scale them.

> I don't know. We have to work on that data.

Howard saw these kinds of simulations as generating in students puzzlement and a sense of incomplete understanding. Students recognized that the problem was an important one with which wildlife biologists had grappled with some success. But they themselves were unsure how to extrapolate from the gold (tagged) jellybeans to an estimated population. In groups, students discussed different approaches. Howard supported and encouraged students' attempts to think about the underlying mathematical ideas, but at no time did she give students the right strategy to use to solve the problem or tell students that they had arrived at the correct answer. This type of socio-intellectual environment, which encouraged students to communicate and reason about their efforts to solve a problem, was unusual among our sample of teachers.

In the following lesson Howard took a more active role in engaging students to think through solution strategies. After all groups had posted the results of their sampling on the board, Howard told students that "we have collected the data but did not analyze it," and recommended that students examine their classmates' data posted on the board. She then referred students to a previous lesson on different ways to scale and compare data, including using percentages, ratios, and unit rates. Students were asked to choose a way to compare data sets and determine the estimated population.

> So that is what we have to do—figure out a good estimate for how many deer are in the jar based on the samples. What do we know about comparisons that allows us to compare what we did in the first sample and what we did in the second sample and what we did in the third sample? . . . Talk with people at your table and read the page in your notebook [on comparing and scaling].

The fact that students chose their method of comparison was important to Howard. Even though the class followed one student's recommendation that they use unit rates, Howard did not try to influence the class' decision.

She took the role of a guide rather than simply a judge of correct responses (Lampert, 1992).

> I knew that they were lost with what to do about the information, and rather than me pushing them in one direction what I decided to do was focus them back on the unit about comparative scaling, and make them refer back to the ideas that we have talked about with comparison, we've talked about ratios and unit rates, and percents. . . . Assuming—assuming wrong—that they would pick out percents as a way to compare the different samples. And they chose to use unit rates, which took me by total surprise as a way to compare the different samples to each other. . . . I didn't know if it makes sense to them . . . to be able to make reasonable predictions about the total population.

In the conversations that followed, students struggled to understand how to use unit rates to figure out how to move from the samples of gold and white jellybeans to an estimate of jellybeans in the jar. Howard expected students to make reasonable predictions, which is why she persistently asked them to explain how they arrived at answers. One group seemed to have figured it out. (Note: All names of students in this chapter are pseudonyms.)

> JASON: Our unit rate was 22.6 and we thought that there was about 2,260 beans.
> JENNY: How did you find the unit rate?
> JASON: We added all our tagged and nontagged deer and came up with 677 and 30 and then divided 677 into 30 and got 22.6.
> JENNY: Okay.
> HOWARD: Does this explanation work?
> KYLE: Yep. They tried to find the unit rate, which is the number of beans divided by colored beans.
> HOWARD: Jill, what exactly does the unit rate mean?
> ERIK: That for every gold bean you have 22.6 normal beans.
> HOWARD: I have another question for you that you do not have to answer right away. How can you compare sample 1 to sample 4? Just think about that. Let's go to another group.
> JAY: What we did was find a unit rate for each of the scoops. For the first sample it was 1 deer for every 18 deer. The second one was 1 for every 16. For the third, we got 1 for every 13.8. For the fourth, 1 for every 12. And for the last, 1 for every 13.
> LANE: How many were in the jar total?

JAY: Our group did not get that far.

HOWARD: Look at what they got for their unit rates. What do you think about the different samples? Do they compare?

AMBER: They compare. As you get more scoops you get more beans.

MEGAN: Some samples were closer together, for example, 4 and 5.

HOWARD: Did other groups find the same results? [students are silent] You are to be talking with each other about how to get the unit rate, and then compare the whole population. Why are we doing unit rates? Where is it getting us?

LANE: I don't know.

AMBER: It isn't helping us. It's kinda hard to figure out the whole jar because you can't multiply each by 100.

HOWARD: You're objecting to using unit rate, but I don't think everyone understands it.

Groups of students were clearly at different points. Some groups had calculated the unit rate for each sample but had not calculated one for all the samples; other students had calculated a unit rate for all the samples and had even arrived at an estimated population. However, no group had yet explained why unit rates provided a useful strategy (one among several) for arriving at the estimated population. Howard recognized that some students did not understand what unit rate was and therefore would be unable to explain how it could be used to arrive at a population estimate.

I thought it maybe would be useful for them to struggle with this, and I think for some of the kids, this made sense to use this idea even though it was difficult to think about. . . . Besides, I wanted them to have a chance to either succeed or fail. Because I think that is worthwhile to try an idea and go with it and say, "Oh, that didn't work," and revise.

Her next move was to help students understand what unit rate meant in one student's formulation that the "unit rate was 22.6 and we thought that there was about 2,260 beans."

HOWARD: How will unit rate help me figure out the total population?

ALEX: I don't know.

HOWARD: Go to the board [where the group's unit rate and total population are posted] and Sarah, you help.

SARAH: 22.6 white beans for every gold bean. 22.6 x 100, and that's about how many beans are in the jar.

JOEL: I agree with that. It's an overall rate for all the scoops.

HOWARD: Where does the 100 in the equation come from? Why do I take this 100 to get the total population?

CARLA: We had 100 gold beans, and we divided by 100 to get a unit rate—1. And to find the unit rate you have to . . .

HOWARD: But what is the 100 beans you are multiplying by? Does this make sense? How do you explain it? Think about this for a minute.

TARYN: In the 100/2,260, the 100 stands for gold beans.

Of course, a key issue is why multiplying the average unit rate of the five samples by 100 leads to the estimated population. Students had arrived at an answer but had not explained the significance of the 100 gold jellybeans in solving the problem. Once again, at the lesson's end, Howard did not provide students with the explanation but expected them to reason their way to it with guidance from her and in consort with classmates.

To compare Howard's teaching with that of other teachers in our sample, it may be useful to characterize more sharply her efforts to teach in light of reformers' ideas. Howard approximates the reform ideal in many respects. The task, which took center stage over several lessons, introduced a real-world problem that intrigued the students and served as the context for them to learn mathematical concepts and procedures. The problem was open-ended, with students proposing different ways to solve both the population grid introductory activity and then the deer population simulation. Howard also treated the task so that students communicated and reasoned about their mathematical ideas and solutions. They were expected to communicate about mathematics by explaining the significance of their sampling results. And they attempted to reason about how to use unit rates to extrapolate to an estimated population. This kind of classroom discourse is critical. Unless students are encouraged to talk mathematics and reason and provide justification for their thinking, they will be unable to construct mathematical knowledge in the manner reformers recommend. In Howard's classroom, students commonly were seen as arbiters whose reasoning was valued in the pursuit of what counted as a better approach or solution to a problem. She noted, "It was very typical that they were working in groups, we shared ideas, and we were trying to collect as realistic information as possible to analyze the situation and then to generalize from it."

Howard did not, however, spend much time, as perhaps reformers would recommend, in the initial, preparatory phase of the lesson evaluating students' proposed solutions to the population grid before she launched into the deer population problem. Students were asked to revisit the range of possible solutions to the population grid problem without discussing whether some strategies would be more appropriate to use than others. Also, after students had completed the activity in which they drew samples, Howard permitted students to choose their own method of solving the problem using unit rates. Before proceeding with the lesson, Howard might have encouraged students to examine the advantages of using one method over another to estimate the population.

These issues notwithstanding, students seemed not so much uncertain about what method to use to solve the problem, as genuinely puzzled about how to use the method to arrive at an answer, including the significance of the 100 gold jellybeans. Howard clearly had created the sort of learning community in which students present and explain mathematical ideas that are then challenged and evaluated (Ball, 1993; Lampert, 1992). Real-world problem solving was intended to be an engine of conceptual advance in Howard's classroom, even if the kind of reasoning was not as extensive as reformers recommend. But even when students had difficulties understanding what to do next, Howard did not give students an answer. She refocused them on the central issue: If they were to understand the solution, they needed to explain why multiplying by 100 provided the estimated total population. Her teaching, although reflecting some weaknesses in the ways described, nevertheless closely approximated the reformers' vision.

A fourth-grade teacher, Ms. Land (pseudonym) took a different tack by tying mathematical content directly to students' daily lives. As she stated: "I try to use real-life situations as much as possible because when they are working just with numbers, it doesn't stay with them; they need to apply it." Scholars (Floden & Buchmann, 1993) have expressed caution about closely tying students' daily lives and instructional content. Students run the risk of failing to achieve the kind of conceptual elevation reformers recommend. But Land's lessons suggested that the risk was negligible, at least in her classroom.

On one occasion, for example, she asked her fourth graders to write stories that represented a division problem. The next day, she said to the class, "Yesterday I wrote a problem on the board, 132 divided by 16. We tried to come up with situations that represented the meaning of the problem in real-life terms." As she spoke, the overhead projection showed division problems and solutions that students had completed the day before:

1. 132 Tootsie Rolls divided by 16 kids = 25 Tootsie Rolls with 8 left.
2. 132 cookies divided by 16 kids = 8 cookies each with 4 remaining.
3. 132 chairs divided by 16 chairs in each row = 8 rows with 4 remaining chairs.
4. 132 people divided by 16 drinks = 8 drinks with 4 left.

But before her 22 students evaluated the story problems, Land asked them to divide into groups of three and then again into groups of seven. Students moved around the room for each activity before Land initiated a discussion.

> LAND: What did we do?
> KAREN: We had 22 kids divided by 3 groups which gave us 7 groups with 1 remaining.
> LAND: Did you divide into or by?

On several occasions during the lesson, Land asked students to be careful about the mathematical language they used. She continued:

> LAND: What was different about the two different sentences: 22 is divided by 7 and 22 is divided by 3? They had the same form.
> ALISON: Oh, I see now. In the second one we had 7 groups and in the first one we had 3 groups.
> CHRIS: I don't understand yet.

What was notable about Land's question and the students' responses is that they illustrated how she introduced the comparison of the two problems to foster students' understanding of division. Alison's response is evidence that at least she was thinking about the problem in the direction Land wanted, and Chris was willing to admit he did not yet understand.

Land then returned to the students' story problems on the board. What was telling about the next series of events was that students spent time trying to make sense of the problems, offering other real-world examples and discussing whether their solutions were defensible. Students were not simply learning a procedure for two-digit long division, but were also discussing the concept of division or the merits of a particular process or solution for a division problem. Land devoted a large portion of the class time to students' reasoning and communicating about the story problems. For example, one student raised the question of whether the last example on the overhead projection made sense. "The sentence should read 16 drinks divided by 132 people. But I don't know how to do this one." Later, a student raised a question about the first example. "I want to go back to the first problem. I disagree that 132 Tootsie Rolls divided by 16 kids equals 25 Tootsie Rolls with 8 left." Other students gave examples not on the overhead, which were examined and often corrected.

Students in Land's classroom were interested both in whether their solutions made sense mathematically and in whether the solution made sense in the real world.

> KERRIE: There are 16 kids and 132 suckers. How many suckers does each kid get?
> SASHA: Kerrie, what's the division problem or sentence? I mean, what divided by what in numbers?
> AARON: 132 suckers divided by 16 kids equals 8 suckers with 4 remaining.
> LAND: Kerrie, do you agree?
> KERRIE: Yes.
> ABLE: 132 parrots in the forest and 16 pythons. How many parrots did each python eat? It equals 8 parrots and 4 remaining.
> LAND: Does this make sense?
> TERI: Is it pythons or parrots remaining?
> CHRIS: Like a parrot would eat a python!

Land also mentioned that she wanted students to see symbolic representations of their story problems when students discussed them with classmates. Referring to the lesson, she stated:

> When they are talking about a problem, I try to write it up (on the chalkboard), so they are seeing the symbolic representation of whatever it is that they are telling about the situation. So I try to model that so they see. Like division: They are not real familiar with the division sign, but they saw that a lot today with all of those problems, and so I should probably have them do some of that [writing the sign], too, now.

In the final phase of the first lesson, Land gave students another division problem that was tied to a real-world application. "Mr. Wilson is in charge of ordering pop for the spring school picnic. He'll need 480 cans of pop. If he buys it in cases of 24, how many cases will he need?"

Once again, students first tried to make sense of the problem.

> TAMI: I tried to multiply 480 times 24 to get my solution.
> LAND: Did anyone in the class multiply?
> KELLI: The answer is 11,520.
> SUSAN: That's not possible [as the solution].

Susan then explained why she did not believe so large a number was a reasonable solution.

In contrast to most other teachers in the sample, Land used a form of mathematical problem solving to expose students' misunderstandings about division and to build on students' existing knowledge. In the initial phase of the lesson, Land attempted to engage students in thinking about the concept of division, using problems whose dividends remained the same but divisors differed.

> I wanted to get them more involved in actually dividing the class up, so that they are using their bodies to divide up into seven groups of three and then three groups of seven. Which is another difficult idea for them to separate. So they are going to be working on really just a couple of division problems that we are going to talk a lot about and try to help them understand.

Then Land attempted to engage students in defending their own division stories. Land mentioned in the postobservation interview that she probably should have permitted students to devise story problems based on a range of division problems, and thus avoided the sometimes repetitive nature of students' explanations and solutions. Despite this weakness, the task centered around students making real-world sense of mathematics. Students talking about mathematics and the use of a range of mathematical representations were central components of her lessons.

While Land's classroom differed from Howard's in the manner in which the real world entered, the mathematical content and pedagogy of Land's lesson were also not a far cry from reformers' recommendations. Both teachers had resolved a fundamental issue for those interested in making mathematics meaningful to students. Not only were their mathematical tasks tied to the real world or students' everyday life, but the treatment of those tasks showed that students were thinking about ideas and procedures that were mathematically important. What Lampert (1992) has characterized as responsible and effective mathematics teaching was reflected in both teachers' attempts to make mathematics relevant to students. Students were learning what it means to know mathematics through their participation in activities that were genuinely mathematical and, in particular, in the sorts of discussions accompanying and following these activities. Although perhaps students were not quite thinking like mathematicians, they were indeed being asked to think about mathematical problems and ideas that were "mathematically fertile" (see Hiebert et al., 1996). Real-world mathematics in these teachers' classrooms probably had the power to motivate students and help them see its usefulness. But what made the lessons mathematically important was that students left the familiar terrain of everyday life to explore mathematical relationships that they had not considered before.

This entry into unknown mathematical territory after students' consideration of features of their daily lives was more apparent in Ms. Yarrow's (pseudonym) seventh-grade classroom. Her lesson involved what are called polygonal tessellations. Tessellation in mathematical terms is the covering of a geometric plane without gaps or overlaps using congruent plane figures of one or more types. In everyday life, tessellation is the way a mosaic floor or wall is covered with squares or other shapes of ceramic tile, stone, or glass. Students would be expected to explain the mathematical idea that underlies patterns found in nature and in cultural artifacts. As Yarrow described it to the researchers:

> There are patterns and relationships that occur in nature and in real life and reasons why people use certain shapes to tessellate. . . . [T]here are reasons why we use certain shapes to quilt, and there are reasons why we use certain shapes to make a tile on the floor. . . . And one of the reasons—one of the underlying math things—is that it is 360 degrees around a point, so that is why certain shapes work. So you could have more than one shape to fit around a point. It doesn't have to be all triangles or all quadrilaterals, but the sum of their interior angles has to be 360.

Yarrow asked her students to name patterns that they saw around them before they responded to the tessellation problem located entirely within the mathematical domain. One student pointed to artwork depicting tessellations on the bulletin board. But Yarrow said that she wanted something from real life. Another student volunteered, "Tree." The exchange continued:

YARROW: Maybe I should be more specific. I want you to give me a
    pattern.
CARRIE: Bathroom floors.
APRIL: Beehive.
YARROW: Good. Good.
FRANK: Railroad track.
YARROW: Where on the tracks?
FRANK: Where those lines are equal.
MICHAEL: [turning to the student who said railroad tracks] Underneath the railing.
YARROW: Anyone else? My grandmother made them.
RACHEL: Quilt. I am so smart.
YARROW: Have you ever seen them? Maybe your Dad makes quilts

since some men do. Have you ever seen them cut out the pattern
of quilts?

RACHEL: Yeah, I have seen them cut out a pattern.

While students clearly recognized patterns in nature and were, in fact, able
to create tessellated artwork, they did not yet understand the underlying
mathematics. As Yarrow put it, "They know how to make them [tessel-
lated drawings], but don't understand why certain polygons tessellate and
why certain ones will not." Yarrow expected that students would draw
upon mathematical terms learned previously.

> They are going to have to remember what an acute scalene triangle is
> and what an isosceles or equilateral triangle [is]. They are using some
> terminology that they are probably going to remember from before.
> But the real idea of this is for them to investigate and make a conjec-
> ture. And from this they are going to see if they can design a tessella-
> tion using more than two shapes. . . . Anybody can tessellate one
> [shape]. And probably anybody with as much effort can tessellate
> two. But I want to see if they can come up with more.

The emphasis on student conjectures after an activity in which students manipulated concrete materials was unusual among our sample of
teachers. Yarrow organized students into groups of four and gave each
group a set of envelopes, each of which contained a different kind of a
cut-out paper polygon. Students first attempted with success to tessellate
equilateral triangles and quadrilaterals. Yarrow then gave each group an
envelope containing a host of irregular triangles. "[I wanted] to get them
to make a conjecture about triangles. To get them to understand that a
triangle can tessellate no matter what the shape is."

After Yarrow found out whether students understood the difference
between scalene, obtuse, isosceles, and acute triangles, she asked students
to "test and see if you can tessellate any sort of triangle. . . . Draw it on
the [tracing] paper and show whether it tessellates." As students worked,
she moved around the room to observe their activity and to answer and
raise questions. A short time later, she asked students in groups to offer
their conjectures to the whole class.

> YARROW: Look up here. You all took a different triangle. What did
> you find out? I know that you had a little problem with your
> tracings.
>
> JODI: Almost any triangle can be tessellated . . . if you use the same
> triangle.

MARIAH: And the same point, edge, or end [of the triangle when you do your tracings].

YARROW: [Standing at the front of the classroom, turns on the overhead projector.] If you were going to make a conjecture about triangles, what would it be?

ALAN: Any triangle can tessellate if you use the same triangles.

YARROW: [Writes down what the student says on the overhead.] How many degrees in a triangle?

LEIGH: 180.

YARROW: How about a quadrilateral? I have here [in these envelopes] scalene quadrilaterals. All the sides are unequal.

After the students had explored whether the irregular quadrilaterals tessellated, Yarrow asked once again about the mathematical explanation for their discoveries.

YARROW: What happened?

TRICIA: They fit together. They all just did.

YARROW: How many degrees in a quadrilateral?

KATE: 360.

YARROW: Explain why there is no gap or overlap.

BOBBI: There is [a gap or overlap].

YARROW: No, there isn't.

TINA: If you have each corner labeled as a different color, and use [measure] one of each color [angle], they all [angles] add up to 360.

YARROW: Why does that work?

TINA: The dot is like a circle, and they fit all the way around.

YARROW: 360 degrees. Why do triangles work?

RACHEL: If you cut . . .

YARROW: If you cut off the corners of the triangles, you see will that it is 360 degrees. But why?

RACHEL: It just is. That's just the way life is . . .

YARROW: Do you think that any polygon can tessellate?

CASS: Yes.

YARROW: Why?

Yarrow then called on two students whose silence suggested that they did not, as others did not, understand the fundamental idea. She also called on several other students. But at a key point, Yarrow seemed to short-circuit students' thinking by providing the explanation. The exchange continued:

CASS: They all have corners, so you always can do a circle around it. . . . How many triangles could you tessellate around one point?

CRAIG: Six.

REBECCA: Seven.

LORI: Twelve.

YARROW: Twelve? Who had the equilateral triangles? All the angles here are how many degrees? Here is the point [where the triangles meet]. Each one of these angles [was] 60 degrees. How many were there? Six. So this one was 360. If you looked at the triangles on the other one, you'd find they added up to 360 degrees.

Mathematics reformers would likely disagree with Yarrow's response at a point when students were struggling, although with limited success, to understand the underlying idea. Rather than have students wander around in the territory of mathematics tessellations, Yarrow herself explained why the triangle tessellated. Later, she commented on her own behavior in relation to the students' conjectures: "Sometimes I let them make a statement and then I let them see if that is a true statement. And sometimes it is, and sometimes it isn't. And sometimes I even get impatient."

To her credit, Yarrow did not give students the overarching mathematical idea she hoped that they eventually would discover themselves: Only those polygons tessellate whose interior angles add up to 360 degrees. Rather, she involved them in another activity in which they tested whether a range of other polygons not previously tested (an equilateral pentagon, hexagon, octagon, decagon, and dodecagon) tessellate. Students were expected to measure the interior angle of each, determine how many of each type of polygon could be placed around a single point, and determine whether a gap or overlap existed. As students became involved in the activity, Yarrow passed from table to table asking questions: "What's the measure of the interior angle?" "How many triangles in a pentagon?" Some students had trouble measuring the interior angles of the polygons. For example, several groups had trouble determining that the interior angle of the pentagon was 108 degrees, meaning that it would not tessellate. In the interview, Yarrow recognized that students were having trouble.

But they will have to investigate hexagons because then they will have to know how many angles will go around the point, which will be 360. So I will let them do that. I will probably have to go back and show them what I am talking about when I talk about interior angles and [show them] what it is they don't understand. But then I am going to say, "Okay, here is the assignment. You are going to have to make a tessellation, and I want you to use more than two shapes. And it is going to have to reflect a pattern [be composed of a repeating pattern], and you are going to have to explain to me why those three shapes are going to tessellate together. And that is going to be the evaluation of it." So they have a designing lesson and they are going to have to do something in writing.

Yarrow's task and her treatment of it represented another way of connecting mathematics to the real world in a manner clearly approximating the reforms. Rather than students working on a real-world problem as in Howard's class, Yarrow initially contextualized the mathematics by referring students to mathematical patterns in the real world. Students then worked on a mathematical problem placed wholly within the domain of mathematics, using concrete materials to test whether all polygons tessellated. Yarrow did not believe that students' use of manipulatives was sufficient to facilitate students' understanding of the underlying idea, a belief Deborah Ball (1992) found prevalent among teachers. Yarrow, in addition, expected students to explain what happened and why as they attempted to tessellate the polygons. With some difficulty, she attempted to elicit conjectures from students and evaluate their thinking, although the kind of extended reasoning in which reformers hope teachers engage students did not occur either at the beginning of the lesson before students engaged in the hands-on activity or after it. Key, of course, would be whether Yarrow would be able to engage students in a further discussion on why the other polygons tessellated or why they did not, and whether students could apply this understanding to their works of art.[1]

BUILDING SCHOOL DISTRICTS' CAPACITY TO SUSTAIN INTENSIVE PROFESSIONAL DEVELOPMENT

All the elementary and middle school teachers in the sample agreed that it is important for students to understand how mathematics is used in the real world. Yet, most teachers rarely made mathematics relevant in the ways recommended by reformers. While all teachers attempted to introduce a real-world problem or make some sort of real-world connection, only 4 out of 25 teachers who said they expected students to reason about mathematics then created a context in which students could do so. Students in these four classrooms were expected to engage in the kind of conjecturing, reasoning, and defending of mathematical ideas and solution strategies that reformers encourage.

The good news is that another 11 teachers in the sample introduced ambitious tasks that seemed to reflect reformers' vision. The tasks suggested that these teachers were attempting to make problem solving a centerpiece of the curriculum and attempting to connect the problems to the real world in a defensible way. Even though teachers in the group of 11 proceduralized the tasks in order to guide students to the right answers, many of their tasks seemed to be in the direction of the reforms (see Spillane & Zeuli, 1997). Of course, the sort of mathematical thinking that reformers recommend was not prevalent in these classrooms, nor did the teachers expect it to be. And it was not clear that these teachers understood how far they had to travel in order to guide students to think rather than simply to provide right answers. The other 10 teachers in the study reinforced a narrow view of mathematics as they attempted to make mathematics relevant to students. The focus on practical skills and naked computational problems, interspersed with occasional real-world problems whose solutions require the whole-cloth application of known procedures, seems a time-honored tradition among many teachers.

It bears restating the argument of reformers that all students can learn to reason about mathematics. The NCTM Standards state specifically that the recommended teaching and learning are not for a select group of students. Among the four teachers in the first group, three mentioned that their classrooms included students who, for a variety of reasons, seemed to have difficulty learning mathematics. Yet the focus of their lessons for all students remained reasoning about mathematical ideas or procedures.

What kinds of opportunities were created for these four teachers to gain a new way to understand their subject matter and to learn a new repertoire of teaching approaches that reflected the reform initiatives? It is clearly not sufficient for teachers merely to introduce mathematical content that reflects a real-world problem or connection. And it is not sufficient for teachers to include a wide range of concrete materials and pictorial representations to teach mathematics, or to use a combination of whole-class, small-group, and individual instruction. These practices were evident among a wide range of teachers in our sample, although only a handful were teaching in ways that approximated the reforms. How did the four teachers learn to rethink and change their teaching of mathematics?

Yarrow, the middle school teacher who introduced the tessellation problem, altered her understanding of subject matter and learned new teaching approaches in relative isolation. Although her district administration supported the mathematics reform, its efforts focused almost entirely on surface features of the reforms, such as whether certain mathematical topics were being taught. There was little, if any, emphasis within the district on making substantial changes in teachers' understanding of mathematical topics and altering how they taught mathematics. Yarrow, however, possessed a strong personal commitment to helping students understand mathematics because of her own experience as a learner. She had always considered herself without innate mathematical ability, but she began to grasp the power of mathematical ideas as part of her undergraduate preparation in mathematics education. This experience enabled her to become increasingly competent as a learner of mathematics and as someone learning to teach mathematics. Motivated by her undergraduate success, Yarrow sought out learning opportunities offered outside her district. She participated in statewide, year-long mathematics inservice projects, regularly attended national and state conferences supported by NCTM, read professional teaching journals related to mathematics, and had begun a masters degree program with an emphasis on mathematics teaching. Yarrow was an unusually ambitious learner who took the initiative to step outside the boundaries of her school district in order to construct rich learning opportunities that changed her fundamental beliefs about what it meant to understand and to teach mathematics.

In contrast to Yarrow, the three other teachers whose teaching approximated the reforms worked in the same school district, which we call Riverville. These teachers had the strong support of district administrators and worked with other mathematics teachers across the district. Riverville had undertaken notable efforts to support teachers' learning about the substance of the mathematics reforms over an 8-year period. Specifically, Riverville school district formed a partnership with mathematics educators at a local university to support in-depth learning about the mathematics reforms. Teachers, teacher leaders, administrators, and university academics worked together to understand what the reforms meant for the teaching and learning of mathematics within the district. With the help of its university partners, Riverville brought curricular materials in line with its reform initiatives through piloting innovative middle and elementary school mathematics curricula. The school district/university partnership supported summer workshops on mathematics content and pedagogy related to the NCTM Standards. The partnership established peer coaching in schools, in which teachers had the opportunity to observe other teachers who were reforming their practice. Also, the partnership encouraged informal associations of teachers around mathematical practice, such as study groups in mathematics. Riverville teachers spoke of extended opportunities to understand mathematical content and pedagogy in ways that challenged their thinking. They spoke of opportunities to observe other teachers engaged in reform practice, and ongoing support for their efforts to learn teaching repertoires associated with the mathematics reforms (see Spillane & Zeuli, 1997; Thompson & Zeuli, 1999).

The contrast is striking between the support the Riverville teachers had from their school district and the lack of support that Yarrow had within her own district. As we consider why most ambitious efforts at school reform have left only a momentary trace, the Riverville example suggests that a school district can provide effective leverage for sustained educational change among a number of teachers within a district. The Riverville teachers described in this chapter were not risk takers or early adopters, who usually take up reforms early on with little prodding. They were not remarkable self-starters, as was Yarrow. Riverville, however, had forged a coherent strategy for implementing a new vision for mathematics education (see Spillane & Thompson, 1997). It had provided teachers with long-term support as they learned new ideas about content, learning, and teaching. No other teacher in our sample spoke of the kind of sustained, within-district opportunities that existed in Riverville for professional development related to the mathematics reforms. Because Riverville had built in the capacity to provide teachers with intensive professional development directly related to the mathematics reforms, we think that it provides insight into how to widen the implementation of the reforms among teachers within a district.

CONCLUSION

This chapter raises a concern besides the obvious one that teachers' reports of what and how they teach on surveys such as TIMSS does not capture the actual progress of the reforms. Our concern is that even though they believe that they are making mathematics relevant, teachers may be reinforcing a narrow view of mathematics and failing to engage students in thinking about mathematical concepts and procedures. By describing the actual patterns of teaching among teachers who both approximate and distort somewhat the reform ideal, we hope to promote a broader recognition of the enormous possibilities and potential pitfalls in making mathematics relevant. Edward Joyner, executive director of the Yale School Development Program, put it best in the following remark made to us during a meeting about the relationship between curriculum and urban, minority students. Joyner (personal communication, 2002) would say to students: "Master what is relevant to you and expand your mind to master the content and skills that have relevance in the larger world so that you don't become irrelevant." Teachers need to start where the children are in order to help them ultimately master the content and skills that have relevance in the larger world. How do teachers learn where the children are? Prolonged observation is one important way. Talking with other adults about the children is another way. Perhaps the most effective way is by communicating directly with the children. The teachers in our sample who most closely approximated the reform ideal were the ones who learned about the children through in-depth discussions with them about mathematical concepts.

NOTES

The research reported in this chapter was supported by a National Science Foundation Statewide Systemic Initiative Grant (Grant No. OSR-9250061) to the Michigan Department of Education, with a subgrant to Michigan State University. Interpretations and opinions offered here do not necessarily reflect the views of the NSF or Michigan Department of Education. The observations and interviews on which this chapter is largely based were conducted by Angie Eshelman, Loyiso Jita, James Spillane, Charles Thompson, Kyle Ward, and John Zeuli. Jennifer Borman joined Jita, Spillane, Thompson, Ward, and Zeuli in preparing analytic memoranda from observation reports and interview transcripts. Errors of interpretation or other flaws in the chapter are, however, solely the responsibility of the authors.

1. Yarrow's second lesson (with eighth-grade students) was quite different. The task involved a real-life problem. Students were slated to go on a field trip to an island where they would have 3½ hours to engage in a variety of activities of their choosing (e.g., go to a butterfly house, to a haunted house, horseback riding, and so forth). Because the island was large, having about a 10-mile perimeter, Yarrow wanted students to plan their activities and the time it would take to walk to the location, attend or participate in the activity, and move on to the next before it was time to leave the island. She also had included an aspect to the problem in which students had to calculate the cost of the activities in which they chose to participate. But the lesson had a narrow, utilitarian focus. Yarrow stated that "the purpose was for students to have some kind of basis for them to see how far it was around the island so they can manage their time." There was no new mathematical idea introduced during the lesson. This sort of narrow, utilitarian purpose associated with practice using previously learned mathematical procedures was common among teachers, although it was unusual for a teacher's lessons to differ materially in terms of their mathematical content and pedagogy. We determined whether the knowledge a teacher emphasized in her mathematics practice was concept-oriented or procedural, based on the more reform-oriented lesson.

REFERENCES

American Association for the Advancement of Science. (1993). *Benchmarks for science literacy*. New York: Oxford University Press.

Ball, D. L. (1992, Summer). Magical hopes: Manipulatives and the reform of math education. *American Educator*, pp. 14–18, 46–47.

Ball, D. L. (1993). With an eye on the mathematical horizon: Dilemmas of teaching elementary school mathematics. *The Elementary School Journal*, 93(4), 373–397.

Cobb, P., Wood, T., & Yackel, E. (1993). Discourse, mathematical thinking, and classroom practice. In E. A. Forman, N. Minick, & C. A. Stone (Eds.), *Contexts for learning* (pp. 91–119). New York: Oxford University Press.

Davydov, V. V. (1975). Logical and psychological problems of elementary mathematics as an academic subject. In E. G. Begle, J. Kilpatrick, J. W. Wilson, &

I. Wirszup (Eds.), *Soviet studies in the psychology of learning and teaching mathematics* (Vol. 7, pp. 55–108). Chicago: University of Chicago Press.

Dewey, J. (1933). *How we think*. Boston & New York: Heath.

Dewey, J. (1956). *The child and the curriculum*. Chicago: University of Chicago Press. (Original work published 1902)

Dewey, J. (1963). *Experience and education*. New York: Collier Books. (Original work published 1938)

Dewey, J. (1965). The relation of theory to practice in education. In R. Archambault (Ed.), *John Dewey on education: Selected writings* (pp. 313–339). Chicago: University of Chicago Press. (Original work published 1904)

Floden, R., & Buchmann, M. (1993). Breaking with everyday experience for guided adventures in learning. In M. Buchmann & R. Floden (Eds.), *Detachment and concern* (pp. 34–49). London: Cassell.

Hiebert, T., Carpenter, T. P., Fennema, E., Fuson, K. C., Human, P., Murray, H., Olivier, A., & Wearne, D. (1996). Problem solving as a basis for reform in curriculum and instruction: The case of mathematics. *Educational Researcher*, 25(4), 12–21.

Lampert, M. (1986). Knowing, doing and teaching mathematics. *Cognition and Instruction*, 3(4), 305–342.

Lampert, M. (1990). When the problem is not the question and the solution is not the answer: Mathematical knowing and teaching. *American Educational Research Journal*, 27(1), 29–63.

Lampert, M. (1992). Practices and problems in teaching authentic mathematics. In F. Oser, A. Dick, & J. L. Patry (Eds.), *Effective and responsible teaching: The new synthesis* (pp. 295–313). San Francisco: Jossey-Bass.

Martin, L. (1990). Detecting and defining science problems: A study of video-mediated lesson. In L. Moll (Ed.), *Vygotsky and education: Instructional implications and applications of sociohistorical psychology* (pp. 372–402). Cambridge: Cambridge University Press.

National Council of Teachers of Mathematics. (1989). *Curriculum and evaluation standards for school mathematics*. Reston, VA: Author.

National Council of Teachers of Mathematics. (1991). *Professional standards for teaching mathematics*. Reston, VA: Author.

National Research Council. (1996). *National science education standards*. Washington, DC: National Academy Press.

Rutherford, J. F., & Ahlgren, A. (1990). *Science for all Americans*. New York: Oxford University Press.

Simon, M. (1986). The teacher's role in increasing student understanding of mathematics. *Educational Leadership*, pp. 40–43.

Spillane, J., & Thompson, C. (1997). Reconstructing conceptions of local capacity: The local education agency's capacity for ambitious instructional reform. *Education Evaluation and Policy Analysis*, 19(2), 185–203.

Spillane, J. P., & Zeuli, J. S. (1997, March). *The mathematics reforms: Mapping the progress of reform and multiple contexts of influence*. Paper presented at the annual meeting of the American Educational Research Association, Chicago.

Thompson, C., & Zeuli, J. (1999). The frame and the tapestry: Standards-based reform and professional development. In L. Darling-Hammond & G. Sykes (Eds.), *Teaching as a learning profession: Handbook of policy and practice* (pp. 341–375). San Francisco: Jossey-Bass.

Thompson, C., Zeuli, J., & Borman, J. (1997, March). *The science reforms: Mapping the progress of reform and multiple contexts of influence.* Paper presented at the annual meeting of the American Educational Research Association, Chicago.

Vygotsky, L. S. (1962). *Thought and language.* Cambridge, MA: MIT Press.

Vygotsky, L. S. (1978). *Mind in society.* Cambridge, MA: Harvard University Press.

ADDITIONAL READINGS

National Council of Teachers of Mathematics. (2000). *Principles and standards for school mathematics.* Reston, VA: Author.

Prawat, R. S. (1991). The value of ideas: The immersion approach to the development of thinking. *Educational Researcher, 20*(2), 3–10.

CHAPTER 3

Mathematics and Science Readiness and Policy

Veronica A. Roberts

WALK INTO THE TYPICAL CLASSROOM of any urban city in the United States, talk to the superintendent of any typical urban school district, or listen to conversations of parents, teachers, and businesspeople at any urban parent–teacher conference or school–community outreach, and the problem of equipping students for the technical demands of the twenty-first century will immediately become apparent. The need for getting students adequately prepared for a marketplace that increasingly needs more people who are literate in mathematics- and science-related fields is rapidly becoming clear. The challenges of preparing students in mathematics and science are especially considerable for low-income urban school districts. There the students' academic needs are greater and teachers are not prepared for providing students with a fiercely competitive program of academic studies. How policy makers, educators, parents, and business leaders address the urgency of these challenges will determine, ultimately, whether or not we succeed in having our students mathematically ready for the demands of an increasingly more rigorous technological society. Students who are equipped with a good grasp of mathematics and science and who are socially and emotionally developed have immense potential for success in tomorrow's workplace.

It is fundamental that the larger educational community has some responsibility to help schools meet the challenges of preparing students, especially those in urban school systems, for the workplace. The current spate of public policy discussion and debate about issues such as curriculum needs, academic standards, and teacher training suggests a promising beginning.

USING SOCIAL AND EMOTIONAL DEVELOPMENT TO PROPEL LEARNING IN MATHEMATICS AND SCIENCE

This chapter is organized around research-guided approaches to classroom teaching and learning. These approaches provide helpful suggestions that schools may use to construct mathematical and scientific meaning for solving problems through practical application to everyday situations. This chapter aims to give educators a fresh understanding of the relationship between social and emotional learning and students' capacity for mathematical reasoning. Instructional support systems and their importance in helping teachers prepare students for the inherent challenges of higher-order mathematics and science teaching and learning also are discussed.

To formulate a workable understanding of how social and emotional developmental factors influence mathematics and science learning, we can look to the theoretical explanations of Ben-Avie and colleagues (Chapter 1, this volume); Resnick (1986); and Madhere (1989). Ben-Avie and colleagues' concept of lifepath reorientation operates on the premise that youth development is active and usually is propelled by adult intervention (by the classroom teacher) and by the social influences of group interaction and teamwork. Ben-Avie and colleagues explain further that acts of learning speak to the active nature of youth development, which often is expressed through active student participation. In classroom events, for instance, we often find that when students think actively about concepts, the process tends to ignite the necessary developmental experience for analytic reasoning. In their study on poor minority children, Resnick, Bill, Lesgold, and Leer (1991) illustrate the importance of this active-thinking-aloud approach in the hands of an effective teacher. Quite often this approach serves to satisfy the social aspects of peer-group needs and thereby yields good returns by building students' emotional comfort with advanced mathematics. In effect, it allows the thinking process to be made visible so teachers can intervene to improve faulty or ineffective thinking patterns in a meaningful way.

Madhere (1989), in his paradigm on the human intellect, calls attention to the importance of actively engaging the students' sense modality preferences in the learning tasks. The level of mental arousal for learning improves when the sense modality of verbal communication is fully engaged in the task.

The concept of lifepath reorientation supports this active engagement of students' verbal intelligence in learning. In this book, we recognize that these theories explain the importance of combining active and reflective thinking and active-participant learning. Therefore, the daily experiences that students gain from classroom activities should be geared to prompt students to think through and reflect upon concepts within an interactive group setting under the guidance of an adult. Instructional support systems should aim to help teachers understand and use the active-participant approach to build student capacities for understanding the "how" and "why" principles for greater mathematics and science learning.

Against this theoretical background, this chapter highlights an inner-city school district in order to establish a context for exploring essential elements of mathematics and science teaching and learning. Existing barriers to success in mathematics and science classrooms are discussed within the framework of practical solutions. The chapter enumerates ways in which informed policy decisions, working in sync with staff development modules and attention to the social and emotional development of students, can ensure that schools do a better job of helping students learn mathematics and science.

THE CASE OF ONE URBAN SCHOOL DISTRICT'S MATHEMATICS SCORES

In the 1980s, one urban school district had a persistent decline in mathematics test scores at the secondary level. Students were doing well up to sixth grade. Thereafter, the scores got progressively worse through eleventh grade. District officials and school administrators agreed that action should be taken, so I designed a comprehensive evaluation of the secondary (grades 7–12) mathematics program (Roberts, 1988).

In this evaluation, our research team asked whether the decline in test scores was related to the quality of the teaching in the mathematics classroom. We theorized that the rapidly declining test scores of the inner-city students might be explained by the type and quality of instruction students were receiving—and not by demographic or socioeconomic factors that typically are given as explanations for low levels of academic performance among inner-city students. A representative sample of classrooms from seventh to twelfth grades was selected to participate in the study. With the aid of a Teacher Observation Checklist for Secondary Mathematics Teachers (developed and validated with assistance from the mathematics department of the urban school district and a series of videotaped models or examples of mathematics lessons), a group of 10 mathematics specialists and instructional supervisors visited mathematics classrooms. Mathematics instructional practices were coded in conjunction with the Observation Checklist based on the following questions:

- How effective was the teacher's questioning behavior to help students understand hard-to-grasp mathematics principles?
- Did the teacher use graphics, pictorials, and concrete objects to explain abstract concepts?
- Did the teacher help students to reason with manipulatives (physical objects) to get at the more hard-to-grasp mathematics principles?
- Did classroom practices include inductive and deductive reasoning? To what extent, for instance, did the teacher provide classroom experiences in (1) the classification of a particular case under a known

general concept in mathematics, and (2) the identification of some general mathematics concept from a particular case?

- Was there repeated evidence of teacher-illustrated examples to aid student understanding of a mathematics principle?
- Did the teacher help students understand problem analysis and problem solving?
- Were the students fully engaged in gainful activities, with wasted time kept at a minimum?
- Where appropriate, were students given opportunities to use calculators, to make estimations, and to apply the skills learned to real-life situations?

The data analysis showed that the quality of instruction (1) successfully predicted high school students' mathematics performance, and (2) reasonably explained the declining mathematics test score patterns.

A barrier to success for many inner-city school students is the defeatist attitude of ascribing blame for the failure of disadvantaged students to urban societal conditions. School districts often explain their students' low academic achievement as a legacy of urban poverty. Frequently, however, students who fail academically are themselves victims of a variety of factors unrelated to the limitations of their socioeconomic status. More often, many of these factors are traced to teachers who are grossly ill prepared in the requisite pedagogy and mathematics content area skills.

Only about 30% of the teachers observed in the study were rated as effective. Additionally, as expected, a majority of the students who were taught by teachers who were classified as effective had the highest mean test scores in both computation and concepts and application skills. The evidence also indicated that when group projects were both well conceived and well managed in the instructional setting, students had opportunities to experiment with structuring and restructuring the elements of a given problem to arrive at a variety of possible solutions.

We also found that students tended to have higher mean scores in mathematics concepts and application skills when they were taught by teachers who:

- Employed the active participant model in their classrooms and engaged students in intellectual discourse
- Dialogued with them and explained the interconnections among concepts
- Asked probing questions
- Gave positive feedback
- Valued students' responses and questioning

In the more effective classrooms, teachers made extensive use of verbalization through reasoning aloud. Teachers spent time actively dialoguing with students about problems related to the more abstract, hard-to-grasp concepts and procedures. At work in these classrooms was the actual "thinking-aloud" behavior intrinsic to the tasks (Carpenter, 1980; Driscoll, 1982; Resnick, 1986; Wagner, 1977, 1981). Teachers sought to find out, through effective questioning, how well students understood the underlying principles behind the symbolic notations, rather than focusing exclusively on rule-based algorithmic computational procedures (Carpenter, 1980). In effect, with these thinking-aloud exchanges, teachers were able to (1) detect and correct inappropriate thinking patterns, and (2) explore with students why certain elements of a given proposition worked as they did. Verbal interchanges between teacher and students also inspired more peer interaction. Together, students grappled with the challenges of the learning tasks and came to understand the mathematics principles through a process of guided discovery.

REFORMS INSTITUTED TO IMPROVE MATHEMATICS IN THIS URBAN DISTRICT

In response to our study, the school district has implemented reforms in an attempt to remediate the students' declining mathematics test scores. Reforms have been aimed at both the academic and social and emotional development of the students. The first initiative has been the planning and implementing of a comprehensive performance-based education approach that attempts to bring together curriculum, instruction, and assessment into a cohesive framework of benchmarks and performance targets. The performance-based approach symbolizes a moving away from a focus on rote learning of isolated skills. This new approach supports an instructional prototype that promotes a conceptual understanding of the principles governing the laws of mathematics and science. It encourages classroom practices that give greater real-world meaning to mathematics. It establishes an assessment system that requires students to actively demonstrate an understanding of the material taught by performing a series of tasks that synthesize their knowledge of a given set of principles. It highlights the use of technology to support and accelerate student learning in the disciplines of mathematics and science.

The district also has sought to implement a mathematics-science-engineering program to operate in tandem with general reforms in the system-wide mathematics and science program. The Emeritus Scientists, Mathematicians and Engineers Program initiative brings retired scientists and engineers into the school district's classrooms to introduce students to a range of career opportunities in their fields. Starting as early as kindergarten, students do simple experiments simulating real-world experiences. Students make direct contact with the tools of the mathematicians and scientists. They weigh objects, estimate measures, try out experiments, and do problem-solving activities. Students get to know the individual mathematician or engineer. They learn firsthand about his or her specialty when they take field trips to the facility where the real work is being done. Fourth-grade students, for instance, get a more comprehensive understanding of how electricity is generated when an electrical engineer uses magnets and wires to illustrate the process and then takes them to a power generating station. Similarly, an aeronautical engineer suspends paper planes, built by fifth graders, in an improvised wind tunnel and then takes the class to Goddard Space Center (Roberts, 1992).

The School Development Program (SDP)—a reform initiative conceived by James P. Comer, a Yale University child psychiatrist and associate dean of Yale's School of Medicine—is helping several of the school district's poorly functioning schools with organizational management and teacher training in the acquisition of critically important child development knowledge and skills. In turn, the teachers use that knowledge to help students develop the skills and attitudes they need to succeed. A school governance team coordinates the development and implementation of a comprehensive school plan that fosters a sense of community and a climate conducive to learning. SDP's mental health component addresses student needs and seeks to avert problems. Broad parental participation enables parents to work collaboratively with school staff to promote the academic and social development of students.

Haynes, Emmons, and Woodruff (1998) have reported their research on Comer SDP schools in our school district. The researchers noted that both reading and math performance were positively correlated with SDP effectiveness in a study of 27 elementary schools. Schools in this district with higher scores on SDP effectiveness generally had higher reading, math, and language scores. The relationship of SDP effectiveness to achievement was constant across all three subject areas and for both grade levels included in the study (grades 3 and 6). The researchers concluded that the consistency of this finding indicates that when the SDP process is implemented well, gains in student achievement are likely to result.

The school district takes the view that these initiatives in academic and social and emotional development, working together, in time will produce the desired impact on student mathematics advancement. Already, minority high school students are taking advantage of school–community partnerships and of academic opportunities offered through area universities.

IMPORTANCE OF TEACHER COMPETENCY IN STUDENT LEARNING

We already know that by whatever means—classroom observation, supervisor recommendation, student test scores, or self- and peer ratings—we assess teachers as effective, certain teacher characteristics emerge as critical to the process of effecting and maintaining desired learning outcomes. The evidence is quite compelling that teacher attributes play a significant role in students' academic success. Among these characteristics are (1) good knowledge of how children learn, (2) sound knowledge of the subject matter of the academic discipline, (3) skill in imparting knowledge or guiding discovery in the teaching–learning environment, and (4) high expectations for student success. Studies have borne out that these teacher characteristics work in the mathematics classroom (Carpenter, 1980; Driscoll, 1982; Evertson, 1980; Roberts, 1988, 1990; Wagner, 1977). Characteristics of influential teachers, as described by former students, include scholarly ability and instructional capability (Johnson, 1987). In a student-based, direct-interview study, Johnson found that the overwhelming majority of successful mathematics students interviewed reported that they were motivated toward the learning of mathematics by the competence, interest, and enthusiasm for excellence of their mathematics teachers.

When we determine that our teachers possess the desired characteristics, we must proceed to unshackle them from focusing exclusively on basic skill development and encourage them to teach mathematics as a scientific tool used to solve problems and explain phenomena in the larger physical universe. Researchers and educational practitioners in the mathematics reform movement tell us that effective classrooms function as communities in which students discuss ideas with their peers and in which intellectual risk taking is nurtured and valued; and where students are exposed to meaningful mathematical tasks, rather than tasks that are merely disguised ways to have students practice an already demonstrated algorithm (Stein, Grover, & Henningsen, 1996). Education policy makers may find it useful to embrace mathematics programs that promote greater self-management of students' mathematics and science education. The writings of Stein, Grover, and Henningsen (1996) provide some examples for developing effective self-management of mathematics learning for understanding. Building capacity for mathematics understanding in the classroom will serve, ultimately, to develop students' own ability to engage their thinking processes in ways similar to those used by makers and users of mathematics. Independently, students will be able to frame and solve their own problems, identify systemic patterns, formulate and test hypotheses, and make inferences based on the outcomes of their tests (Stein et al., 1996).

A Talent Development Problem Solving Protocol, designed by the Center for Research on the Education of Students Placed at Risk, provides teachers with another practical tool to promote self-management of students' problem solving (Madhere, 1997). This protocol captures the sequential elements of a typical problem-solving task and makes them available for conceptual understanding and application. It asks and answers a series of important questions, among them: What is your goal? What are you trying to find out? What conditions must be met to accomplish the goal? If we have X, then . . . what? What relevant information is given? What relevant information is missing? How can we arrange all the information into a simple diagram? What mathematical concept does the diagram bring to mind? What formula can we construct for the development of concepts? Once a solution to the problem is found, students must ask the relevant follow-up questions: Does this formulated construct make sense in relationship to the original goal? Can we explain the results briefly and clearly? When we provide students with this generic step-by-step approach to problem solving, we give them a workable tool to help them apply concepts independently in a variety of mathematics- and science-related disciplines.

A RECIPE FOR SUCCESS

Prescriptions for school improvement in disadvantaged neighborhoods have constantly echoed the clarion call for new investment dollars. However, examples from history tell us that more money has not necessarily been the answer. Clearly, there is support for the idea that new resources are needed urgently in many depressed urban communities, but the inference that poverty diminishes children's capacity to excel in challenging academic pursuits runs counter to proven realities. A myriad of cases exist in which schools—public, private, and parochial alike—serving low-income minority children in urban settings excel. Ask Irwin Kurtz, Principal of P.S. 161 in the Crown Heights neighborhood of Brooklyn, New York, how he was able to get children in a school that is 90% Black, 8% Hispanic, 1% Asian American, and 1% Caucasian to achieve the highest reading and mathematics test scores in its school district. Ask him how he managed to take the school's test scores from the bottom quarter of the district's scores to the top (Siegel, 1997). Much of the answer rests with the successful integration of an active parent–community partnership in his school's education program.

This anecdotal evidence provides an excellent example of the fundamental reasons for many of the successes that have been achieved in disadvantaged urban communities. Chief among these reasons are:

- Effective classroom management where teachers are held accountable
- A robust and highly competitive academic curriculum of studies coupled with challenging academic standards and high expectations for student success
- A rigorous program of academic instruction
- Deep discussion in the exploration of mathematics and science concepts and their relationships to real-world situations
- A sound school–parent alliance grounded in a clear, well-enforced discipline policy with zero tolerance for student behavior that undermines learning

Essentially, these factors have little to do with whether the child is poor or wealthy. To declare that urban poverty is the cause of student academic failure is clearly an excuse designed to mask the ineptitude of many school districts' weak curricula and ill-prepared classroom teachers. Having a vision for a school that embraces and marshals support for high-quality academics and social and emotional development constitutes the recipe for the ultimate success of schools.

REFERENCES

Carpenter, T. (1980). Research in cognitive development. In R. J. Shumway (Ed.), *Research in mathematics education*. Reston, VA: National Council of Teachers of Mathematics.

Driscoll, M. (1982). *Research within reach: Secondary school mathematics*. Columbus: Ohio State University. (Eric Document Reproduction Service No. ED 225 842)

Evertson, C. H. (1980). Predictions of effective teaching in junior high school mathematics classrooms. *Journal of Research in Mathematics Education, 2,* 167–168.

Haynes, N. M., Emmons, C., & Woodruff, D. W. (1998). School development program effects: Linking implementation to outcomes. *Journal of Education for Students Placed at Risk, 3*(1), 71–85.

Johnson, M. (1987, April). *Success in learning mathematics*. Paper presented at the annual meeting of the National Council of Supervisors of Mathematics, St. Paul, MN.

Madhere, S. (1989). Models of intelligence and the black intellect. *Journal of Negro Education, 58,* 189–202.

Madhere, S. (1997). *A talent development problem solving protocol*. Unpublished manuscript, Center for Research on the Education of Students Placed at Risk.

Resnick, L. B. (1986). *Education and learning to think*. Special report prepared for the Commission on Behavioral and Social Sciences and Education, National Research Council, Learning, Research and Development Center, University of Pittsburgh.

Resnick, L. B., Bill, V., Lesgold, S., & Leer, M. (1991). Thinking in arithmetic class. In B. Means, C. Chelemer, & M. S. Knapp (Eds.), *Teaching advanced skills to at-risk students: Views from research and practice* (pp. 27–53). San Francisco: Jossey-Bass.

Roberts, V. A. (1988). *An evaluation of secondary school mathematics program: A final report*. Washington, DC: District of Columbia Public Schools.

Roberts, V. A. (1990). Relationships among processing behavior mode, cognitive development level and mathematics achievement in black metropolitan high schools students. *Dissertation Abstracts International, 51*(106), 5054.

Roberts, V. A. (1992). *Emeritus scientists, mathematicians and engineers (ESME) program: A final evaluation report SY 1991–1992*. Washington, DC: Emeritus Foundation.

Siegel, J. (1997, October 8). The jewel in the crown. *Education Week*, pp. 25–29.

Stein, M. K., Grover, B. W., & Henningsen, M. (1996). Building student capacity for mathematical thinking and reasoning: An analysis of mathematical tasks used in reform classrooms. *American Research Journal, 33*, 455–488.

Wagner, S. (1977). *Conservation of equation and function and its relationship to formal operational thought*. (Eric Document Reproduction Service No. ED 14117).

Wagner, S. (1981). Conservation of equation and function under transformation of variable. *Journal of Research in Mathematics Education, 12*, 107–117.

CHAPTER 4

Developmental Pathways to Mathematics Achievement

Judy Bippert & Nadine Bezuk

THIS CHAPTER DISCUSSES HOW the Yale School Development Program (SDP) enhances mathematics instruction. We begin by summarizing the idea of the developmental pathways within the SDP educational change initiative. We then present recommendations based on our experience of enhancing students' learning and development in schools that serve diverse student populations. We conclude with some examples of activity-based learning experiences—games—that may be used by teachers or parents.

THE SCHOOL DEVELOPMENT PROGRAM
AND THE DEVELOPMENTAL PATHWAYS

James P. Comer, associate dean of Yale's School of Medicine and founder of the Yale School Development Program, designed a model for school improvement based on principles of child development. When Comer, as the head of a team from the Yale Child Study Center, intervened in two schools in New Haven in 1968, he was dismayed by the chaos, friction, and tension he observed between and among students, staff members, and parents. His dismay, in great part, stemmed from his awareness of the potential for the community when there are strong home-school links: "Schools can be invaluable in spearheading the community's economic achievement, in repairing its social fabric, and in preparing schoolchildren to continue to improve the community in the future" (Haynes et al., 1996, p. 47). In response to the complete disarray and confusion that surrounded him in these schools, Comer drew on his training in psychiatry and public health to conduct a problem analysis. In addition to his theoretical analysis, Comer reflected on his own experiences growing up and realized that the seamless, intertwined fabric of community that supported his own development was missing in the lives of the students he encountered. So he resolved to reinvent community in schools.

For the school staff, parents, and community members, reinventing community meant engaging in three primary activities: writing a comprehensive school plan, aligning staff development with the plan, and designing ways to assess and modify the plan. For the students, reinventing community meant engaging in cooperative, authentic, and purposeful school and classroom activities that promoted community (Comer, 1997). When such activities are commonplace—and when there is stability and continuity of adequate leadership and teaching in the school—good test performance results.

When explaining child development to parents and school staff, Comer employs the idea of six developmental "pathways"—physical, cognitive, psychological, language, social, and ethical. The idea of the pathways is a metaphor, which enables school communities to look at themselves and students through the lens of child development. Through learning about how to promote the development of their students, staff members themselves grow. School communities become centers that promote adult human development and, in turn, the development of the children.

As activities, games provide an entry point for adults to impact the development of children (the topic of this chapter). Comer tells the story of a young boy who wanted the ball of another boy. The adult intervened by spelling out the options other than popping Johnny in the mouth. Comer writes that the adult intervention helped the child "grow along all of the critical developmental pathways" (reprinted in Comer, Haynes, Joyner, & Ben-Avie, 1996, p. 16) because the adult's intervention went far beyond just solving the immediate problem.

In the classroom, the SDP promotes social and emotional learning, including self-control, negotiation, and conflict management skills, along with academic achievement (Comer, 1980). The aim is to build positive, communicative, and caring relationships with and among students to boost academic success.

The SDP has much to contribute to enhance mathematics instruction for all students. We can increase students' self-confidence and analytic thinking by organizing instruction to include interesting activities to develop concepts and reinforce skills. While there are few lessons that can meet all the aspirations of the math standards and SDP guidelines, with careful selection and planning, teachers can gather a collection of learning experiences that meet these expectations in interesting and challenging ways. Here are some examples of how the expectations for mathematical achievement can intersect with the social and emotional developmental pathways. Concrete materials give students a physical model to use. The interactions with others provide students with opportunities to practice social skills and give teachers a golden opportunity to reinforce the use of consensus, collaboration, and no-fault—the three guiding principles of the Comer Process. In the classroom, consensus means that loud or dominating students are not allowed to intimidate other students; collaboration instead of competitiveness is the norm among students; and no-fault means that students are not blamed for being born into certain families or ethnic groups. Students need to take responsibility for their own behavior, supporting the ethical pathway. Interest in the activities helps develop positive attitudes toward mathematics, building on the psychological pathway. The cognitive pathway is strengthened through learning the mathematical skills. Solving word problems enhances the development of the language pathway. The developmental pathways, combined with parent support and rich mathematics investigations, provide many resources to increase students' mathematics learning.

In San Diego we have added a seventh pathway to Comer's metaphor of the six developmental pathways. Our seventh pathway is the psychocultural, which helps us to address the range of cultures and language groups in our community. Children and adults are working toward better understanding of the many cultures in the city and ways to support the learning of students from all cultures.

How can we use developmental knowledge to enhance the learning of mathematics? Table 4.1 shows some of the ways each of the pathways can be addressed.

WHAT WE HAVE LEARNED ABOUT ENHANCING THE MATHEMATICS LEARNING OF ALL STUDENTS

In San Diego, we conducted a longitudinal study that looked at implementation of the Comer Process and student academic success. Each year in the 4-year study, students, parents, and staff at 12 Comer schools and eight control schools completed surveys on school climate, classroom environment, and implementation of the Comer Process. In Borton, Preston, and Bippert (1996) we present data that show that students' improvement in mathematics achievement may be predicted by their sense of caring teachers who maintain high expectations for learning and a well-disciplined classroom. In Borton, Preston, and Bippert (1998) we describe the continuation of the longitudinal study, which shows that the Comer Process is an effective strategy with students in schools that serve diverse populations. The following is a brief review of the study:

To give an accurate report of progress of Comer schools, it is important to note that the 12 schools, which serve approximately 11,500 students, have diverse student populations and are in different geographic communities. Eleven of the schools are elementary and one is a middle school. A total of approximately 5,700 students, 390 teachers, and 1,110 parents completed surveys in the spring of 1995. In the spring of 1996, 5,200 students, 540 teachers, and 3,000 parents completed the surveys. In the spring of 1997, 5,500 students, 700 teachers, and 1,500 parents completed the surveys. Students completed school climate, classroom environment, and social competence surveys. Staff members completed school cli-

Table 4.1. Mathematical Implications for Developmental Pathways

Pathway	Definition	Mathematical Implications
Cognitive	Acquisition of basic knowledge and flexibility of thought	Providing plenty of reasoning tasks—the challenging sort that promote thinking and leave children feeling a sense of accomplishment when they find a solution
Psychological	Feelings of self-adequacy and ability to manage internal states	Displaying a positive attitude toward mathematics and understanding the importance of mathematics for everything we do in life, since teachers and parents have a great influence—positive or negative—on how children perceive mathematics
Social	Ability for empathy and interaction	Giving opportunities for students to work and talk together using the SDP's three guiding principles (consensus, collaboration, no-fault)
Language	Receptive and expressive skills	Oral and written communication about work in mathematics, including explanations about the process used for solving problems and why the solutions make sense
Physical	Physical health and nutrition	Using concrete materials or physical activity to support understanding of mathematical concepts
Ethical	Awareness of norms and respect for self and others	Having children assume responsibility for their own learning
Psychocultural	Respect for a multitude of other cultures	Working well with others of all cultures; having high expectations for all students

mate, teacher efficacy, and SDP implementation surveys. Parents completed school climate surveys.

Analysis of 1995 and 1996 survey data suggests that continued, significant efforts by schools to improve school climate, parent involvement, and teacher efficacy are important components in any strategy to improve student achievement in math. Analysis of pre- to post-treatment (1994–95 to 1995–96) student performance on the Stanford Achievement Test Series, Abbreviated (Math Applications) indicates positive gains for high-implementing SDP schools when compared with low-implementing and control schools.

Our experience in teaching mathematics to diverse student populations has shown us the importance of implementing a school reform process that promotes shared decision making. In San Diego, the results are clear: Student performance in mathematics may be predicted by the students' sense of self-confidence, perceptions of mutual trust and respect, and perceptions of a well-disciplined classroom. These qualities are promoted when schools consider how students work together, how learning activities can best stimulate learning, how responsibilities are given to students, and how families can support learning. We have developed the following recommendations, based on our experience and research, for teachers and parents to keep in mind to enhance the mathematics learning of *all* students:

1. Build on students' previous learning because learning is developmental.
2. Teach for understanding: Teach concepts and meaning before drill and practice.
3. Consider learning styles of students: Use various modes of representation, including auditory, visual, and tactile (manipulatives).
4. Maintain high expectations for achievement regardless of gender or ethnicity.
5. Foster a supportive, nonthreatening learning environment.
6. Encourage students to talk and write about mathematics.
7. Use cooperative groups: Assign and rotate roles to enhance the status of low-status students.
8. Use equitable questioning techniques: Randomly direct questions to students/allow for equal response opportunities; equitably distribute difficulty level of questions; use equal and adequate wait-time.
9. Relate math to students' everyday lives.
10. Support good study habits and hard work.
11. Point out importance of math for careers.
12. Involve parents and the community: Establish and maintain posi-

tive relationships with parents; provide specific suggestions and materials for students to take home to enable parents to support classroom instruction and student learning; reward students with extra points for completing math homework that involves working with family members.

COLLABORATING WITH PARENTS

As we found in our research, parent involvement is an important component in any strategy to improve student achievement in math. Parents have important perspectives about their children that may help school staff in their efforts to educate the students. Most parents truly care about their children, especially parents who may have experienced educational failure themselves. Parents often need to have schools take the initiative in helping them understand the various roles they can play in their children's education, especially in mathematics. Socioeconomic status and lack of education have no effect on the willingness of parents to help their own children.

Parent Expectations for Mathematics

The way math currently is taught is probably different from the way most parents and many teachers were taught 20 or 30 years ago. Parents generally see mathematics as a rigid set of rules to be memorized. Effective mathematics classes, activities, and assignments should include hands-on experiences that are likely to excite and encourage youngsters. Since parents expect that the math their children are learning will be beneficial and applicable to life outside school, schools need to help parents understand that the way math currently is taught is helping their children be successful in life outside school as well as inside school.

Strategies for Helping Families Support Student Learning in Mathematics

- *Homework*. Ensure that homework is meaningful and related to learner outcomes, and that parents are aware of the connection. Frequently provide interactive projects that involve family members. Be sure to offer parents the tools and information they need to make homework a successful experience. Provide information on assessment as well as curriculum and instruction.
- *Letters or calendars for families*. Descriptions of specific classroom mathematics activities, paired with suggestions for support, help keep

families aware of upcoming projects and ways in which they can support their children's learning. This is a good chance to explain the importance of the topic and how it relates to academic goals and everyday life.

- *Back-to-school night.* This is an opportunity to foster goodwill and support for a partnership with parents throughout the year. Acquaint parents with academic goals and planned math activities. Encourage family involvement in home mathematics projects. Play a few games showing how students can practice mathematical facts so parents can see the importance of playing games at home.
- *Family math nights.* These are afternoon or evening events centered on math. Families attend together and participate in math games and activities that they can continue at home with their children to support their learning.
- *Home activities.* Activities that involve parents and/or siblings increase understanding among all parties. Teachers can send these home periodically, making sure to send activities that do not require costly or hard-to-find materials. For special projects, teachers also can ask for materials to be donated for sharing with families unable to purchase their own.

These strategies are fairly easy to implement but have a positive impact on students' mathematics learning.

ACTIVITIES TO SUPPORT STUDENTS' MATHEMATICS LEARNING

The nationwide movement for high standards has determined what students should learn, and also has mandated that students demonstrate what they know. In a balanced, rigorous mathematics program, students need to become proficient with basic skills, develop conceptual understanding, and become adept at problem solving. The games in the following sections provide engaging activities that promote students working in a social situation, practicing skills, and thinking about outcomes. They are also appropriate for home activities with parents.

Challenge Card Game

There are many forms of the game War. This one provides practice for multiplication and addition; children use concrete materials, social skills, self-responsibility, and oral communication. It is an opportunity to help students deal with a competitive situation and still preserve caring, positive relationships.

Materials needed: 36 playing cards, four each of the numbers 1–9, paper and pencils for each player to keep score.

Number of players: 2–4

Game rules:

- Each player draws one card from the stack. The player drawing the lowest number is the dealer.

- The dealer shuffles the cards and deals out two cards face up and one card face down to each player. Players multiply their two face-up cards and add the face-down card to the product.

- The player with the highest total wins the round and scores 10 points.

- The player to the left of the dealer becomes the next dealer and shuffles the cards. All players are again dealt two cards face up and one card face down, which they multiply and add as before. The winner is the player with the highest total and scores 10 points.

- The game continues with the players taking turns being the dealer.

- The winner is the first player to score 50 points or the player who has the most points at the end of the designated time.

Fractured Fractions

People in many cultures have used dice for hundreds of years. This game challenges partners to study probability and practice reducing fractions. One of the important concepts of probability is the idea of fairness. This investigation provides an opportunity to discuss how fairness in a game runs parallel to real-life situations.

Materials needed: Game rules, gameboard (any gameboard will do as long as there are at least 20 spaces to move), game markers, one set of dice for each pair of students, pencils and blank paper for recording outcomes.

Preparation for the game: Give each pair of students one set of dice. Explain how to create a fraction less than one with dice. This is a good time to reinforce students' use of mathematical vocabulary, for example, "The numerator must be smaller than the denominator to make a fraction less than 1." You also may need to review how to reduce the fractions that they will create. Before beginning play, have students predict the outcome of the game and why they made that prediction. This could be a math journal entry.

Game rules:

- Decide which player will be player A and which will be player B.
- Roll the dice. Create a fraction less than 1 by using the smaller number as the numerator and the larger number as the denominator. For example, if you roll a 5 and a 3, make the fraction three-fifths, which is less than one. If the numbers are the same (doubles), roll again.
- Record each fraction on a recording sheet, including the "doubles."
- If the fraction can be reduced, player A moves one space. If it cannot be reduced, player B moves one space.
- Play this game several times, taking turns being player A and player B.

Create a class graph with all the possible fractions on the bottom. Have each pair of students record the results of their games on the graph. After all the results of their games are recorded, you may want to circle those that can be reduced so students actually can see the difference in the possibilities. There are 30 possible ways to create a fraction, excluding the doubles. There are eight ways to create a fraction that can be reduced.

Is the game fair? It is possible to make this game fair if player A moves 11 spaces when the fraction reduces and player B moves 4 spaces when the fraction doesn't reduce. The idea of "fairness" provides the opening for conversation in the classroom to promote positive attitudes in competitive situations. (Adapted from *Game Factory*, by Bippert & Vandling, 1996.)

Popsicle Probability

The idea of using decorated game sticks comes from Native American games. An exploration into fair outcomes, this activity allows children to interact socially in a constructive way designed to create positive attitudes for mathematics and responsibility for learning. Use of concrete materials, appreciation of Indian culture, working with others, and problem-solving skills are incorporated.

Materials needed: Game rules, gameboard (any gameboard will do as long as there are about 20 spaces to move), game markers, three popsicle sticks or tongue depressors for each student, colored markers, pencils and blank paper for recording outcomes.

Preparation for the game: Give each student three game sticks. Students will use only one set of three for the game, but they will need their own set to take home to share the game with their families. Have them decorate one side only. You may want to suggest that they use an Indian design. If you have limited time, it would be helpful to have the sticks decorated ahead of time.

Demonstrate to students how they are to use the sticks. They are not to throw them. They should hold all three sticks upright in one hand about 1 foot above the table, then drop them onto a flat surface. They will advance on the gameboard depending on what sides of the sticks come up. Before beginning play, have students write about their prediction of the outcome of the game (which player will win, A or B) and why they made that prediction.

Game rules:

• Decide who will be player A and who will be player B.

• Place your markers on the start of the gameboard.

• Take turns tossing the three sticks at the same time.

• Player A will move two spaces if all the sticks land with their design side up, and one space if all land with their plain side up.

• Player B will move two spaces if one stick lands with its design side up and the other two are plain, and one space if the sticks land with one plain side and two design sides up.

• Play this game several times, taking turns between being player A and player B, and recording (by making a tally) which player wins each game.

Make a class chart of which player wins most often in each pair. Player B should win more than player A because of the unequal probability. Students will need to be shown how to figure out all the different ways there are for the sticks to land. There are eight possibilities. Player A has a ⅜ chance of moving spaces and player B has a ⅝ chance of moving, but things are further complicated because sometimes they move one space and sometimes they move two. So another way of looking at this is that when the sticks are dropped eight times, player A theoretically should move three spaces and player B should move nine spaces. This game is not fair! In class discussion, have students present their ideas on how to make it fair and explain why their way would work. (Adapted from *Game Factory*, by Bippert & Vandling, 1996.)

CONCLUSION: ACTIVITY-BASED LEARNING EXPERIENCES

Brophy and Alleman (1990) observe that in the process of implementing curricula, teachers spend most of their time "managing the classroom and motivating students, presenting information and demonstrating procedures, asking questions and engaging students in content-related discourse, introducing and scaffolding student progress on activities and assignments, and evaluating student learning" (p. 1). Most of these enduring and fundamental aspects of the teacher's role have been the focus of sustained scholarly analysis and research. Yet, Brophy and Alleman (1990) continue, "This has not been true of activities and assignments, however, despite their virtually universal perceived importance and use in the classroom" (p. 1).

Ben-Avie and colleagues (this volume) explain that activities spark developmental experiences. Student learning is transformed into a developmental experience when students reflect on what they have learned from a math or science activity. Specifically, providing students with developmental experiences is a twofold process: math or science activity + reflection = developmental experience. Math and science activities by themselves are not developmental experiences. Thinking through or reflecting on the activity, under the guidance of an adult, is a necessary component of the developmental experience. On the other side of the equation, without the solid content (the new knowledge) of the activity, students have nothing to reflect on. When an engaging activity is combined with thoughtful, guided reflection, then teachers are helping students have a developmental experience.

REFERENCES

Bippert, J., & Vandling, L. (1996). *Game factory: A simulation in which pairs of students investigate probability by determining the fairness of games*. Carlsbad, CA: Interaction.

Borton, W. M., Preston, J., & Bippert, J. (1996). *Validating the Comer model: The effects of student, teacher and parent affective variables on reading and mathematics performance outcomes*. Paper presented at the annual meeting of the American Educational Research Association, New York.

Borton, W. M., Preston, J., & Bippert, J. (1998). *Sustainability of reform imple-*

mentation in Comer schools: Measuring the impact of change in a shared decision-making model. Paper presented at the annual meeting of the American Educational Research Association, San Diego.

Brophy, J., & Alleman, J. (1990). *Activities as instructional tools: A framework for analysis and evaluation* (Occasional Paper 132). East Lansing: Michigan State University, College of Education, Institute for Research and Teaching.

Comer, J. P. (1997). *Waiting for a miracle: Why schools can't solve our problems— and how we can.* New York: Dutton.

Comer, J. P. (1980). *School power: Implications of an intervention project.* New York: Free Press.

Comer, J. P., Haynes, N. M., Joyner, E. T., & Ben-Avie, M. (Eds.). (1996). *Rallying the whole village: The Comer process for reforming education.* New York: Teachers College Press.

Haynes, N. M., Ben-Avie, M., Squires, D., Howley, P., Negron, E., & Corbin, J. (1996). It takes a whole village. In J. P. Comer, N. M. Haynes, E. Joyner, & M. Ben-Avie (Eds.), *Rallying the whole village: The Comer process for reforming education* (pp. 42–71). New York: Teachers College Press.

CHAPTER 5

Success for Minority Students in Mathematics and Science: Prerequisites for Excellence and Equity

Dionne J. Jones

It is important for policy makers to realize that systemic, ecological changes need to occur to ensure that minority students succeed in mathematics and science. In an effort to discuss some of the prerequisites for programs for minority students, this chapter will first describe several successful programs and then present a model for successful mathematics and science education.

STRATEGIES THAT WORK

A number of programs have been developed to provide greater participation by African American and Hispanic students in mathematics and science beyond primary school. Such programs may be cultivated through the collaborative efforts of schools, parents, churches, community-based organizations, and the business community. The intervention strategies utilized by these programs reflect various elements of the model of success for minority students that are presented in this chapter.

Middle School Talent Development Project

Recognizing that the transition from elementary to middle school may be risky for many students, researchers with the Center for Research on the Education of Students Placed at Risk at Howard University developed a talent development framework based on the belief that all students can learn challenging material. The model is based on two key elements of effective schools, namely, instructional infusion in the curriculum and support for learning. Instructional infusion in the curriculum provides students with a foundation in English, mathematics, science, and social studies, and continues with materials and activities designed to expand critical thinking skills. Support for learning is provided through activities that involve cognitive skills and provide motivational experiences. Cognitive skill development includes after-school tutoring, magazine subscriptions, and a summer enrichment program at the university. Motivational activities include a self-assessment checklist, interest assessment, career fair, academic recognition, and family affirmation and cultural empowerment (Madhere, 1997).

Putting Parents in the Plan

This program was developed by the Parent Resource Center of the New York Urban League with a grant received from the State Education Department to "support school success through the professional development and education of public school parents" (New York Urban League, 1997, p. 1). The major goal of the program is to help parents become more informed and better prepared to address changes in federal, state, and city policies designed to raise educational standards. Parents attend a series of seven workshops that provide strategies for enhancing learning both inside and outside school. Workshop topics include: asking the right questions; building a partnership with teachers to support learning; sustaining important dialogue with teachers about curriculum, homework, and meeting standards; using community resources to enhance learning; and utilizing new computer technology to expand parents' knowledge as well as support their children's learning. Workshop speakers are affiliated with organizations in the community, thereby providing parents direct linkages to other community agencies that support children's learning. While parents are in the workshops, their children are engaged in a computer-assisted learning program that exposes them to a broad range of educational software designed to build their skills in core academic areas such as mathematics and science.

PRIME Universities Program

The PRIME Universities Program recruits minority students from public, parochial, and private schools in the Philadelphia, PA, and Camden, NJ, areas. The program consists of five consecutive years of sequential summer enrichment instruction beginning at post-seventh-grade level through post-eleventh-grade level. Programs are offered on college campuses at each grade level and provide intensive instruction in mathematics, communication skills, and science and computer applications. In addition, students receive specialized curricula, individual counseling and tutoring, hands-on career awareness and exploration activities, and a residential experience simulating college life (Strengthening Underrepresented Minority Mathematics Achievement [SUMMA], 1997).

Southeastern Consortium for Minorities in Engineering

Southeastern Consortium for Minorities in Engineering (SECME) is a collaboration of 34 universities and 65 industry/government agencies with 463 schools and 21,014 students. The goal of SECME is to increase the pool of minorities who are prepared to enter and complete studies in engineering, mathematics, and science. Working with students in grades K–12, a SECME team is formed at participating schools to plan and carry out the program. A team typically includes the principal, a counselor, a mathematics teacher, a science teacher, a language arts teacher, and a media specialist. Team members are trained by SECME at a summer institute held for 2 weeks at a different SECME university campus each year and at regional workshops during the school year. SECME member universities offer scholarships to SECME graduates. Overall, more than 91% of graduating SECME seniors attend a college or university and almost half of them choose engineering or other mathematics-based fields (SUMMA, 1997).

San Antonio Pre-Freshman Engineering Program

Organized by the University of Texas in 1979, this program identifies high-achieving minority middle and high school students and provides them with academic enrichment to pursue careers in mathematics, science, and engineering. Students attend an intensive 8-week mathematics-based summer session and study logic, algebraic structures, probability and statistics, physics, computer science, engineering, and technical writing. Abstract reasoning and problem-solving skills are developed through coursework assignments, examinations, and laboratory projects. In addition, students attend career awareness seminars and take field trips to learn about mathematics- and science-based careers. The program participants meet on eight college campuses and at several high schools in the city. More than 6,000 students have completed one summer of the program; 70% have been minority, 54% have been women, and 52% have come from low-income families. The high school graduation rate is 99.9%, and the college graduation rate is 80%. The science and engineering graduation rate is 56% (SUMMA, 1997).

Other University/School Programs

Many colleges and universities attract precollegiate students to mathematics and science by sponsoring summer and weekend outreach programs for high school and middle school students (Carey, 1995). For example, the Florida Agricultural and Mechanical University (FAMU) initiated a 6-week, residential Young Scholars Program (YSP) in mathematics for students entering grades 9, 10, and 11. Through the project, FAMUYSP exposes students to careers in science, engineering, and mathematics. Each student develops a project that will be entered into science fairs and completes a research paper that contains a computer analysis (SUMMA, 1997). Temple

University has a similar program that recruits students as early as seventh grade. Students in middle school participate in an academic program at Temple Medical School for 6 weeks during the summer. Ninth and tenth graders go for 10 weeks during the summer to Temple Medical School to do an apprenticeship, while eleventh and twelfth graders have internships in government and industry (Williams, 2000).

PREREQUISITES FOR EXCELLENCE AND EQUITY

The programs briefly described above are examples of programs that provide excellence and equity. The remainder of this chapter presents a model for success for African American and Hispanic students in mathematics and science. The model includes all forces that impinge on the student—socially, emotionally, and academically. In this ecological approach, the student is seen as one element (at the center) of a larger system. Elements of the system that impact the student socially and emotionally are teachers, parents, peers, the media, and role models. Students engage in academic activities that require cognitive processing. Students' attitudes toward, performance in, and decisions about mathematics and science depend on social, emotional, and academic experiences. Thus, to increase the absolute number of African American and Hispanic students successfully completing advanced-level mathematics and science courses and selecting careers in mathematics- and science-related fields, more positive influences must be present. All of these influences affect students socially, emotionally, and academically and are described in detail below.

Teachers

To expose students to mathematical and scientific techniques and concepts early in their educational life, teachers provide meaningful practical experiences, even at the prekindergarten level. For example, the teacher may use an electric or gas meter to illustrate the functional use of numbers. Similarly, the teacher may include mathematics examples taken from the life experiences of the child that may be as simple as counting the number of pieces in a jigsaw puzzle to ensure that all the pieces are there. In addition to engaging African American and Hispanic children in computational and repetitive drills in the early years, teachers develop students' problem-solving and abstract reasoning skills. This is important at all stages of students' schooling.

Teachers encourage the children to engage in problem solving, not merely drill and practice. Using pedagogical approaches that allow for open-ended responses and alternative solutions, teachers include mathematical games, cartoons, computer programs, and other audiovisual aids in the classroom. By properly sequencing operations and concepts, teachers reduce the chance of failure. By encouraging group interaction, they allow students to learn from one another (Melton, 1996). Such groupwork allows for social interaction among students, which has been found to be extremely effective in classroom learning (Cobb & Mayr, 2000; Elias & Weissberg, 2000; Sylvester, 2000).

A classroom atmosphere that is nonthreatening promotes effective questioning by students. Such an environment promotes the mental readiness for the abstract and higher-order thinking that advanced mathematics requires. Activities in science and mathematics that are based on an experiential model promote student construction of scientific knowledge, and challenge them to make the transition from basic to higher-order, scientific ways of thinking (Tuss, 1996).

However, teachers of mathematics and science, like teachers in other subject areas, sometimes have low expectations for African American and Hispanic students' mathematics and science abilities (Peng & Hill, 1995). In fact, many teachers expect students of low socioeconomic status (from which many African American and Hispanic students come) to fail, and expect students of high socioeconomic status to succeed. Teachers' expectations have been shown to influence student outcomes (Anyon, 1995; Peng & Hill, 1995). As a result of their low expectations for African American and Hispanic students, many teachers tend to adjust their educational goals, teach different material, and even reward and punish behavior differently according to a student's class and race.

Parents

Other factors that may be related to mathematics and science achievement among African American and Hispanic students are the resources and learning opportunities that are provided for them at home. Given that a high proportion of African Americans and Hispanics live below the poverty level, few African American or Hispanic parents serve as role models for their children in science- and mathematics-related fields, or can adequately assist them with science and mathematics homework at the higher grade levels. Few of these parents provide opportunities for their children to engage in educational extracurricular activities such as visiting a museum, zoo, or an art gallery or attending a play or concert (Fouad, 1995; Peng & Hill, 1995). Yet, African American and Hispanic parents hold high educational expectations for their children and need schools to provide these experiences.

A number of barriers prevent many minority parents from becoming fully involved in school. For parents for whom English is not their first language, communication is a major barrier. Such barriers are alleviated when schools have information about school events and activities written in multiple languages, such as is done in Fairfax County Schools in Virginia. Some other barriers facing minority parents are long work hours, limited access to transportation, and babysitting problems. Transportation problems are addressed by organizing car pools or providing other means of transportation to school events. Having older students babysit during school events addresses babysitting problems.

Schools, in collaboration with civic and community-based organizations, can sponsor awareness programs to help parents become more aware of school activities and events. For example, programs can help parents understand the importance of taking time to read and review homework and of giving their children an audience when the children relate their accomplishments and the class activities of the day. High parental expectations for their children, as well as support and encouragement for them to do well, help students develop a positive academic self-concept. Research has shown that students who perceive themselves as having a high level of academic ability in mathematics and science tend to perform at higher levels than students whose perceptions of their own mathematics and science performance are low (Jones, 1988).

Finally, by expressing interest in and concern about their children's education, parents hold teachers accountable for the education of their children. When parents join and participate in parent associations or school committees, they have a voice in the decisions that are made in the school (U.S. Department of Education, 1996).

Peer Groups

Group learning and partner learning encourage students to see themselves as a community of learners (Cobb & Mayr, 2000; Dunn, 1995; Elias & Weissberg, 2000; Melton, 1996; Sylvester, 2000). Research conducted on cooperative learning has shown that making schoolwork social and exciting increases academic achievement as well as intergroup relations (Cobb & Mayr, 2000; Elias & Weissberg, 2000; Sylvester, 2000). When students engage in activities that involve their newly learned science and mathematics knowledge, it helps to solidify the learning. It also provides the opportunity for them to see the utility of mathematics and science as they transfer and apply classroom experiences to out-of-class situations. Experiences such as these help students to develop a positive attitude toward mathematics and science because they see the subjects as beneficial and real (Jones,

1988; Rech, 1994). Through cooperative learning, the enthusiasm of a few students can be transferred to many other students.

Media

The media are critical in raising the level of consciousness of children and communities regarding mathematics and science. Indeed, it was the media that helped to develop and perpetuate stereotypic views and misperceptions of mathematicians and scientists by creating movies such as *The Absent-minded Professor* and *Frankenstein*. Instead, the media could develop positive television, movie, and print images of mathematicians, engineers, and scientists who are African Americans, Hispanics, other minorities, and women. One relatively simple way to initiate this is for newspapers to run daily columns and for television programs to have daily segments on applications and advances in mathematics and science that feature a diversity of people.

Role Models

Currently, there is also a lack of mathematics and science teachers as mentors or role models. In eighth-grade mathematics classes, African American teachers teach 32.5% of African American students, and Hispanic teachers teach 17.6% of Hispanic students. However, White teachers teach 93.9% of White students. The situation is similar in eighth-grade science classes for African American and White students, but a smaller proportion of Hispanic students (7.9%) are taught by Hispanic teachers (Peng & Hill, 1995). This is partially due to the overall smaller proportion of minority teachers. Yet, the lack of role models may indirectly inhibit African American and Hispanic student enrollment and achievement in mathematics and science (Peng & Hill, 1995).

Teachers can invite minority men and women who work in mathematics and science fields to come into the classroom and give brief lectures and interact with students. Leaders and local community members can serve as role models. African American and Hispanic children need to know about national and community leaders in mathematics- and science-related careers to whom they can look for guidance and to whose stature they can aspire to achieve. Biographical sketches of these leaders, developed in school and at home, can provide excellent reading material for students. In some instances, such material will illustrate for students that the background and upbringing of the role models are similar to their own. In this way, many African American and Hispanic students will be able to identify with the role models and thereby increase their self-esteem and motivation to pursue and succeed in mathematics and science.

Mentoring relationships also can be developed between minority students and scientists, with opportunities provided for students to visit their mentors on site at their jobs. This can be an awesome, emotionally charged experience for students, positively impacting their sense of self and creating a desire to be as successful as their mentors by inculcating their mentors' values. Mentoring relationships can be formed with community role models, with the mentoring going well beyond academics to include social and emotional aspects of the students' lives. The desire to please their mentors can be a reinforcing factor in students' desire to learn and to study hard. Role models have to be cognizant of the fact that they are under a looking glass. Their protégés are watching their every move, and attending more to what they do than to what they say. It is a clear case of the old adage, "Actions speak louder than words."

Cognitive Processing

Cognitive processing focuses primarily on the academic, although the way in which it is done also affects students socially and emotionally. This occurs in a continuous manner throughout students' home and school experiences. The student internalizes and processes the messages sent and makes certain decisions about them. The expectation is that messages sent in a positive manner increase the likelihood that they will be received positively. Through guided reflection, the student integrates and synthesizes the learning and experience with teachers, parents, peers, the media, and role models. Although each of the elements in the system affects the student differently and the student relates to each differently, the ultimate message is the same. The net effect that stays with the student is expected to be: I can succeed in mathematics and science; mathematics and science are enjoyable subjects; mathematics and science are meaningful and have practical applications; and the career opportunities offer superior rewards, both financially and cognitively/socially/emotionally.

However, subtle forms of discrimination in school serve to undermine students' social and emotional well-being and eventually push them out of school. Examples include programmatic approaches, such as placing students in special education and Chapter 1 pull-out programs, and organizational approaches, such as ability grouping and grade retention. Both of these approaches have the potential to stigmatize students, decrease opportunities for learning, and provide less stimulating learning environments (Montgomery & Rossi, 1994).

Tracking, or grouping students by ability in schools, also has been found to be negatively correlated with African American and Hispanic students' performance in mathematics and science. As a result of grouping or tracking students, the upper-level courses in many schools continue to consist of predominantly White students, while lower-level course ethnic composition is predominantly African American and Hispanic (Peng & Hill, 1995). Tracking begins as early as elementary school, becomes more marked at the secondary school level, and continues through the educational pipeline into college. An important implication of this distribution for academic achievement is that vocational education students earn fewer school credits in areas such as English, mathematics, and science. Moreover, the course content in the academic subjects in lower tracks is often different from that in the higher tracks. Students in vocational tracks often take general mathematics rather than algebra and trigonometry, and general science rather than biology and chemistry (Peng & Hill, 1995).

One More Issue: Equity in Resources

The lack of adequate resources and materials has a significant influence on students' sense of social and emotional well-being and on their academic performance. Within states, there are patterns of inequitable and insufficient financing that undermine the ability of many communities to fully equip their schools. Some school districts spend more than twice as much money on their children's education as do neighboring districts. Since schools are financed primarily by state and local property taxes, areas with high rates of poverty, unemployment, and underemployment create a low tax base, especially for local governments in many inner cities and rural areas, resulting in low educational expenditures. Moreover, schools in the poorest districts face the double jeopardy of having students who are most at risk and having the least amount of money to implement needed programs for improving the quality of education.

EXCELLENCE IN, EXCELLENCE OUT

If students' social, emotional, and cognitive development have been relatively positive experiences, the expected outcome will include enrollment in advanced mathematics and science classes in high school, excellence in mathematics and science in high school, pursuit of mathematics and science beyond high school, and career choices in mathematics- and science-related fields. In other words, there will be excellence in, resulting in excellence out.

Given appropriate and adequate social, emotional, and academic support, minority students can and do perform at high levels of achievement in mathematics and science (Belluck, 1997; Milne & Reis, 2000). For many of these students, academic success is seen as a victory over adversity because they have overcome the odds and demonstrated their inner strength. As America's public schools continue to search for effective ways to address the needs of their minority students, the approaches to educating these students must incorporate strategies to build student confidence and increase motivation and academic self-esteem, while providing the academic skills needed to succeed.

One result of elementary and secondary inequity, poor teaching materials, low expectations, and poor feedback is seen in higher education. A review of college enrollment rates and the proportion of degrees conferred on African American and Hispanic students illustrates the bleak state of affairs. During the 1990s, the percentage of 18- to 24-year-old African American and Hispanic students enrolled in college increased progressively (Snyder, Hoffman, & Geddes, 1997). However, the proportion of bachelor's degrees in mathematics- and science-related fields conferred on these two groups of graduates did not increase from their previously low level (Snyder et al., 1997).

Without intervention, the impact of these educational experiences will be increasingly devastating on the minority population, as it will further increase occupational segregation by race (Hall & Post-Kammer, 1987). Thus, proactive strategies are required in order to reverse these existing patterns and to prevent the emergence of additional racial disparities. In the next decade, labor studies forecast a higher than average growth in science-related occupations. This is an additional incentive for those responsible for educating African American and Hispanic students to prepare them to be competent in mathematics and science.

CONCLUSIONS AND RECOMMENDATIONS

A number of inequities combine to impede the academic achievement of African American and Hispanic students. There needs to be equitable resource allocation in school districts where these students predominate. In addition to adequate resources in their schools, minority students require meaningful learning experiences with relevant and current materials and equipment. Their teachers must have high expectations for them and provide them with positive feedback. Instruction must engage and challenge students so that classroom climate—and thereby intellectual development—may thrive. Indeed, student interest is a significant determinant of how students attend to and persist in processing information (Montgomery & Rossi, 1994). Minority parents must support their children's efforts. For those parents who are not able or do not know how, the school and community must form alliances to provide support so that these parents can advocate for their children. Teachers, parents, peer groups, the media, and role models must work collaboratively for the good of all students. Partnerships that succeed are a sure way to reach the goal of success for all students.

From a broad national perspective, it is critical that school curricula expand to include more required mathematics and science courses, particularly for African American and Hispanic students. The research evidence suggests that the number of years of mathematics taken and the number of courses of advanced-level mathematics taken are positively correlated with a student's mathematics achievement (Jones, 1988; Snyder et al., 1997). Some strategies include:

- Equalization of per-pupil expenditure by state and local governments to eliminate "rich" and "poor" schools
- Revision of school curricula and methods of teacher instruction so that learning is meaningful, stimulating, and, to the extent feasible, fun
- Development of sensitivity and cultural awareness among teachers through staff development and training programs in order to alleviate the negative effects of racism, sexism, classism, and cultural discrimination
- Provision of in-depth counseling, mentors, and programs to African American and Hispanic students at an early age, even in elementary school, to make them aware of the wide array of opportunities and fields open to them
- Replication of model programs of university or business school partnerships with proven track records of success
- Implementation of the model presented in this chapter in a concerted effort to develop new levels of proficiency in mathematics and science among African American, Hispanic, and other at-risk students

In summary, to achieve the national goal of the United States being a world leader in mathematics and science achievement, drastic educational reform is needed for all students (U.S. National Research Center, 1996). Moreover, given the projections that the more competitive jobs will require higher-level advanced mathematics skills than they do now, it is imperative that educators and policy makers take immediate action to guarantee competitiveness for African American, Hispanic, and other at-risk students (Wei-Cheng, 1995). Thus, as shown in this chapter, a combination of strategies must be used at various levels by government, schools, teachers, and parents to establish a cadre of African Americans, Hispanics, and other at-risk groups in science and mathematics. The political and sociocultural dimensions of schooling must be seriously considered in order for sustained fundamental change to occur in schools (Cooper, Slavin, & Madden, 1997). It is only with comprehensive reform strategies in place that there can be success for all students.

REFERENCES

Anyon, J. (1995). Race, social class and educational reform. *Teachers College Record*, 97(1), 69–89.

Belluck, P. (1997, May 8). More minority students enter elite schools. *New York Times*, p. B.4.

Carey, P. M. (1995). Creating a new generation of black technocrats. *Black Enterprise*, 26(1), 140.

Cobb, C. D., & Mayr, J. D. (2000). Emotional intelligence: What the research says. *Educational Leadership*, 58(3), 14–18.

Cooper, R., Slavin, R. E., & Madden, N. A. (1997). *Success for all: Exploring the technical, normative, political, and socio-cultural dimensions of scaling up* (Report No. 16). Washington, DC: Howard University, Center for Research on the Education of Students Placed at Risk.

Dunn, R. (1995). *Strategies for educating diverse learners* (Fast Back 384). Bloomington, IN: Phi Delta Kappan Educational Foundation.

Elias, M. J., & Weissberg, R. P. (2000). Primary prevention: Educational approaches to enhance social and emotional learning. *Journal of School Health*, 70(5), 186–190.

Fouad, N. A. (1995). Career linking: An intervention to promote math and science career awareness. *Journal of Counseling and Development*, 73(5), 527–537.

Hall, E. R., & Post-Kammer, P. (1987). African American mathematics and science majors: Why so few? *Career Development Quarterly*, 35(3), 206–219.

Jones, D. J. (1988). Factors associated with mathematics achievement and the selection of a mathematics-related or a nonmathematics-related major among African American college students (Doctoral dissertation, Howard University). *Dissertation Abstracts International*, 49(06A), 1410.

Madhere, S. (1997, March). *Talent development in action: Transforming middle and high school.* Paper presented at the annual meeting of the American Educational Research Association, Atlanta.

Melton, J. A. (1996). Does math performance improve when students select their own partners? *Teaching & Change*, 3(3), 244–259.

Milne, H. J., & Reis, S. M. (2000). Using video therapy to address the social and emotional needs of gifted children. *Gifted Child Today, 23*(1), 24–29.

Montgomery, A., & Rossi, R. (1994). *Educational reforms and students at risk: A review of the current state of the art.* Washington, DC: U.S. Department of Education.

New York Urban League. (1997). Brooklyn branch is awarded grant to "Put parents in the plan." *Brooklyn Dialogue, I*(2), 1.

Peng, S. S., & Hill, S. T. (1995). *Understanding racial-ethnic differences in secondary school science and mathematics achievement.* Washington, DC: U.S. Department of Education.

Rech, J. F. (1994). A comparison of the mathematics attitudes of black students according to grade level, gender, and academic achievement. *Journal of Negro Education, 63*(2), 212–220.

Snyder, T. D., Hoffman, C. M., & Geddes, C. M. (1997). *Digest of education statistics.* Washington, DC: U.S. Department of Education.

Strengthening Underrepresented Minority Mathematics Achievement. (1997). *Directory of mathematics-based intervention projects.* Washington, DC: Author.

Sylvester, R. (2000). Unconscious emotions, conscious feelings. *Educational Leadership, 58*(3), 20–24.

Tuss, P. (1996). From student to scientist. *Science Communication, 17*(4), 443–470.

U.S. Department of Education. (1996). *Putting the pieces together: Comprehensive school-linked strategies for children and families.* Washington, DC: Government Printing Office.

U.S. National Research Center. (1996). *Third International Mathematics and Science Study* (Report No. 7). East Lansing: Michigan State University.

Wei-Cheng, M. (1995). Educational planning and academic achievement of middle school students: A racial and cultural comparison. *Journal of Counseling and Development, 73*(5), 518–530.

Williams, M. (2000). *Progress report on the PSTP pipeline study: A report to NIH for the minority research trainee program.* Philadelphia: Temple University.

CHAPTER 6

Nurturing Mathematics Learning in the Classroom

Jacque Ensign

WITH INCREASED RECOGNITION OF THE IMPORTANCE of social/emotional education in the wake of recent tragedies in the United States, those of us who teach in teacher education programs have a challenge similar to the one we have faced with multicultural education. Both multicultural education and social/emotional education often are considered to be add-ons to school curriculum. The danger in each of them being taught as add-ons is that teachers have the impression that these areas are separate from curriculum, rather than part of a larger approach to teaching and learning. This is especially problematic given the changing school population of the United States. Cochran-Smith (2000), in her vice-presidential address to the American Educational Research Association, quotes Gloria Ladson-Billings as asserting that "the changing demographics of the nation's schoolchildren have caught schools, colleges, and departments of teacher education by surprise. Students are still being prepared to teach in idealized schools that serve White, monolingual, middle class children from homes with two parents." In this chapter, I will argue that while traditionally mathematics has not been taught as a subject that fosters the social and emotional growth of students, nor the success of diverse students, it can achieve this when students' personal out-of-school experiences are an integral part of classroom mathematics lessons.

UNDERLYING CONVICTIONS FOR NURTURING MATHEMATICS LEARNING

In order to teach mathematics and science well, teachers need to focus on high-quality content while also tending to students' social and emotional development. For all students to learn math and science well, we believe that the following convictions must be true.

All Children Can Learn Math and Science Well

During the writing of this book, Michael Ben-Avie was interviewing a parent who complained that when her child was failing in math class, a teacher tried to placate her by saying that traditionally 20% of students do not succeed in math and science classes. The explanation was that some kids are smart in math and others are not, and that the parent should just accept that her child was not. If we contrast that scenario with the nation's work-force needs, we see a major discrepancy between the teacher's beliefs and the demands of today's society. We no longer have the luxury of allowing 20% of our students to fail in math. No longer is failing math a problem confined to a school subject; it has societal consequences. If we do not teach all children so that they can succeed in mathematics and science, we are doing a disservice to society as well as to individual students. As Michael Ben-Avie (2001) has shown so graphically in his research on youth development and learning, succeeding in math is not only about under-standing math, but about the whole trajectory of a child's life. Failure in one math class in high school can now be shown to be related to dropping out of high school. As Ben-Avie said to the staff of one school, "If you accept 20% of your students failing math courses, you also have to accept your high drop out rate."

However, lowering standards is not an effective way of ensuring that students do not fail in math and science. One cannot just lower standards, try to make math more interesting, and expect more students to stay in school. As Zeuli and Ben-Avie (Chapter 2, this volume) have shown in their research on teachers, what is relevant is not just math that is connected to students' lives, but math that challenges students to see deeply into math, to get engaged in math. By helping them to see the deep relationships in math, teachers give students a clear message that they think all students can learn well.

All Children Deserve to Learn Math and Science Well

If, as educators, we are really committed to social justice, then not only will we believe that all children can learn well, but we also will embrace the conviction that all children deserve to learn well. If our society is ever to address the inequities in it, we must begin by examining how well we prepare all our children for succeeding in society.

Valerie Maholmes, of the School Development Program, sat in on the recent Carnegie Corporation's task force on learning in the primary grades. She reflects, "We know that public opinion is that we need more testing of children. We were grappling with the fact that we know that these assess-ments are not going to go away. But how can we make sure that they are used not to hurt children, but to support education and development of children?" Maholmes tells the following story in order to underscore the importance of looking at the potential and deservedness of children and not only at their past and their present position in society:

> I am involved with an alternative high school. The students were all in the juvenile justice system for one reason or another. They had

been tossed away by the regular high school. They were told that they could not learn. There was a student in this school who had wanted to spend more time in the computer lab. The teacher talked with him and said, "If you're serious, I'm serious and I am willing to work with you." The teacher told me, "This child is so smart and is so bright, but he presented himself as if he had no skills and no knowledge. But this child intellectually has so much potential and so much capability. If I had not had some sense of what I want these children to work towards, I would have tossed him away as well." I think these children have been the victim of no expectations so much for so long and so often, that we do them a disservice by saying that standards do not apply to urban minority children. We do not have any idea how the relationship that I or you might have with a child might shape that child's life—maybe not right away, but later on.

Social and Emotional Development Are Critical in Teaching Mathematics and Science Content

After years of hearing claims that social and emotional development are important for schools to address, we now have data to support those claims (Ben-Avie et al., Chapter 1, this volume). Math and science are part of overall academic success. This research on youth development and student learning shows strong relationships between students' social and emotional development (coping and engagement with adults) and behaviors that increase the likelihood of academic achievement. A strong relationship between students' learning and their social and emotional development was observed in different student populations ranging from Black and Latino urban students in the northeast to White rural students in the south. In all schools, students' social and emotional skills were strongly related to their problem-solving skills in math and science.

PERSONALIZED MATHEMATICS LESSONS

For students who find school alien to their interests and lives, personalized mathematics lessons can provide the link for them to succeed in mathematics. Zeuli and Ben-Avie (Chapter 2, this volume) note the National Council of Teachers of Mathematics' call for teachers to use real-life examples. In my research in schools in which students are not thriving in mathematics, a problem seems to be that when real-life examples are used, those examples come from the teachers or textbook authors. For students from mainstream cultures, these textbook or teacher problems may be close enough to students' experiences that they can be somewhat effective. But since teachers and authors have very different lives from those of nonmainstream students, what is real life for them is not real life for these students. Neither teachers nor textbook authors tend to know real-life examples that are emotionally involving for these particular students. The result is that students are no more engaged in these fabricated real-life examples than they were in lessons without them. The further away from mainstream culture (and hence from school mathematics) students are, the more important it is for teachers to use their students' actual life experiences, as it helps them bridge to school math. Just as we speak of the importance of teaching students from nonmainstream cultures to code-switch in their speech, so too is it important to teach them how to use their mathematical experiences to help them bridge to the concepts and skills required by school mathematics. Going beyond the utilitarian value of using students' experiences, teachers also have the chance to teach, as Freire (1993) urged, "that lived experience be used as a point of departure so as to transcend it" (p. 109). Ultimately, the hope is that students will gain sufficient school knowledge that they will be able to critically examine their lived experiences and make decisions that will positively affect their lives.

In my research, I found that for real-life problems to engage students who were not in mainstream cultures, the problems had to be specific examples from students' lives instead of what I prefer to call realistic problems—problems that teachers or authors think these students might find relevant. Rather than assuming that any or all of these students share experiences with others who look like them or come from a similar economic background, this approach demands that teachers see students as individuals who bring particular experiences with them to the classroom. This approach challenges teachers not to assume that these students have experiences or interests just because of the culture to which our society assumes they belong. Teachers learn to focus on the particular cultures of these students instead of lumping them into stereotyped cultures. So, when I say we use students' personal experiences, I mean exactly that: experiences that particular students in one classroom have had, not just experiences we think they would have had. To do this demands that teachers draw from their students stories of actual experiences each has had that are emotionally engaging. These have to be experiences that the students care about, that they want to discuss and remember and share with the class.

While some advocates of the National Council of Teachers of Mathematics' reforms in mathematics education may frown on the use of students' personal problems as focusing on utilitarian uses of mathematics, I have found that the academic, social, and emotional effects on students, and even teachers, outweigh the dangers. When teachers particularize mathematics by using students' personal problems, students become involved and interested in mathematics lessons, allowing the teachers to then go beyond the utilitarian aspects of students' problems to focus on the conceptual aspects of mathematics. Without that emotional buy-in, students do not get to the conceptual mathematics, or often even to the procedural.

RELATIONSHIPS ARE KEY IN MATHEMATICS, BOTH COGNITIVELY AND SOCIALLY

In her research to examine the characteristics of successful teachers of African American students, Gloria Ladson-Billings (1992) has identified culturally relevant teaching as one trait shared by these teachers. She has noted how culturally relevant classrooms for African American students foster a sense of community and sharing (characteristic of what this book refers to as social and emotional). My own research has begun to tap into the area of culturally relevant teaching as a way of understanding the relationship between social/emotional development and learning, with the hope of being able to improve content teaching in mathematics for diverse students.

Math is far more than formulas and procedures. Focusing on procedural math is a simplistic view of math and damaging to students if that is all that is taught. That is how math usually has been taught, with only a portion of the students succeeding. In today's society, it is crucial for teachers to recognize that mathematics is ways of thinking, ways of solving problems, ways of understanding our world. Math is about relationships, problem solving, logical thinking, expansive thinking, creative thinking, and seeing patterns—all critical skills for all citizens in today's technological world.

Stigler and Hiebert (1999), analyzing data from the Third International Mathematics and Science Study, noted differences in how math was taught in Japan, where students scored well on the international tests, and in the United States, where students did not score as well. In Japan, the researchers noted that teachers act as if mathematics consists of relationships between concepts, facts, and procedures. Frustration and confusion are expected and are considered to be a part of the learning process. Japanese students learn mathematics by exploration and then discussion of strategies and concepts with their classmates. In contrast, students in the United States are expected to learn procedures. They are given strategies and then are expected to practice them individually. Students in the United States learn mathematics by following rules from teachers and texts, and relationships are omitted in mathematics classes. Then we wonder why so many of our students do poorly in mathematics.

Teachers in the United States also can teach for deeper understanding (Zeuli & Ben-Avie, Chapter 2, this volume). By spending time on in-depth discussions and investigations of a problem, teachers help students understand the relationships between concepts, facts, and procedures. No longer are the students parroting back rote facts and procedures. Fewer computational problems may be solved in such classes, but students' engagement in mathematics and understanding of mathematics are enhanced.

I argue for the value of building communities of mathematicians who develop strong personal and interpersonal relationships with the mathematics being studied. These relationships are emotionally and academically engaging for students, both in helping them develop relationships with others in their class and in helping them see the relationships between home and school mathematics. This puts mathematics within a larger framework of understanding and interpersonal relationships than is commonly done in U. S. classrooms.

SOCIAL AND EMOTIONAL LEARNING IN MATHEMATICS LESSONS

Compared with non-nurturing classrooms, classrooms that foster social and emotional growth have an ambiance of care and concern, allowing members of the class to function with one another as friends. Students feel they have something valuable to add to the class. Students share their personal feelings and experiences with classmates and the teacher, and they feel comfortable doing so. Each person in the class feels heard. Noddings (1992) notes that "knowledge of each other . . . forms a foundation for response in caring" (p. 23). Sharing personal experiences and having those experiences respected is, according to Noddings, key. "We cannot separate education from personal experience. Who we are, to whom we are related, how we are situated all matter in what we learn, [in] what we value, and [in] how we approach intellectual and moral life" (p. xiii).

In mathematics classrooms, who counts socially and emotionally? During a mathematics lesson, besides processing the mathematics, students also are processing social and emotional information and keeping count of that information. Am I smart? Am I good enough to be in this class? If I reveal anything about my life at home and outside this class, what will others think of me? Students gather this information from their interactions with both teachers and fellow students and then act on it.

Teachers, especially of young students, matter. Students are keenly sensitive to messages teachers send to them about their worth. Does the teacher smile at me? Does the teacher care what I do or feel? What does the teacher think of me when I make a mistake or ask for help? These are questions students ask no matter what subject is being taught, including mathematics. In addition, fellow students' relationships with them matter, usually more than that with the teacher. When I ask a question or give an answer in class, how do my classmates react to me? When I work in small groups, do my classmates want me in the group and want my ideas? Yes, teachers and fellow students do count socially and emotionally. When teachers complain that Deshawn is not engaged in mathematics class, is it because of the mathematics itself or is it because of factors more closely related to social and emotional issues for Deshawn? Students keep mental tallies of the answers to those questions that they internally ask about their relationships with teachers and fellow students, making judgments about themselves in the process. Unfortunately, sometimes those judgments are negative and students react by disengaging during lessons.

SOCIAL/EMOTIONAL EFFECTS WHEN PERSONAL EXAMPLES ARE INCLUDED

Intimacy is built when students and teachers get to know each other in caring ways. When a student relates a personal experience of using mathematics, the accompanying story lets classmates and teachers know more about that student's life, including problems and decisions that the student has made. When the teacher introduces a lesson on calculating time intervals to Jasmine's class, he could ask if anyone has gone on a trip where he or she had to read train or bus or plane schedules. Jasmine might volunteer her story of riding a city bus, and the class could then use her information in its calculations. For the rest of the class, Jasmine's personal experience becomes a vicarious out-of-school experience that they can use to link to school mathematics. No longer is calculating time intervals something that happens only in math class. Now the entire class links this classroom math to Jasmine's personal experience riding a city bus.

Penelope Peterson (1994), in analyzing a first-grade classroom, notes that students' sharing of personal experiences helps to build community. "The learning context in Annie's classroom is one of community. Drawing on her work in creating a classroom 'community of readers and writers' in language arts, in her mathematics teaching Annie attempts to help her students see themselves as a community of mathematicians" (p. 63). When students feel part of a community, they are more apt to be positively engaged in lessons.

In previous work (Ensign, 1997), I have explored from an anthropological perspective how intimacy is developed or prevented in lessons depending on the amount of sharing of "gifts." In the case of mathematics classes, if the only knowledge and examples come from the text and the teacher, the exchange of "gifts" of knowledge is only one directional, resulting in low intimacy. Instead, if students' knowledge and examples are included in mathematics lessons along with the text's and teacher's examples, the result is higher intimacy in that class.

Besides the practical pedagogical advantages of using students' personal experiences as meaningful contexts, Dewey (1900, 1916) also advocated a synthesis of students' outside and school lives for societal reasons. He was concerned that schools not be so divorced from students' lives that students lose a sense of community. Students who feel included and valued in their education, who develop ties with others in the classroom, and who learn to respect and have discussions with classmates are experiencing what it is to live in a community. They can then take what they have learned about their microcosm of a community and become engaged in larger communities in society.

CONDUCTING RESEARCH ON THE USE OF PERSONAL EXAMPLES IN MATHEMATICS CLASSES

Over the course of 3 academic years, I conducted research in five inner-city elementary classrooms in two schools. These School Development Program classrooms were selected because the teachers agreed to incorporate students' out-of-school mathematics problems when teaching mathematics topics. Students were observed and interviewed before and after the units in which teachers used students' personal mathematics problems. The teachers taught each topic using personalized problems elicited from the students. For review lessons on the mathematics topics, students wrote and illustrated a personal experience in mathematics to demonstrate how they had used that mathematics outside of school. I spent 1 day a week over the course of the 3 academic years in the classrooms, as a participant observer and as an interviewer, depending on the data being collected. Classroom data consisted of field notes, samples of student work, audiotapes of interviews with each student before and after the intervention, and videotapes of classroom instruction.

Observations, video recordings, and interviews with students and teachers in classrooms incorporating personal experiences show that students have a higher sense of self-worth, and a higher sense of being included and heard in mathematics classes. As an example, one second grader, Tonya, went from being a noncompliant student to very involved during the course of a year in which students' personal mathematics experiences were incorporated into the lessons. During the weeks of pre-intervention, observations of Tonya showed a student who was consistently belligerent and defiant to such an extent that she frequently was dismissed from the classroom during mathematics lessons. After 2 months of the teacher incorporating into lessons students' personal experiences, including hers, on a regular basis, Tonya was one of the most eager participants in math lessons. She wanted to share her experiences so much that she was willing to behave well in class, to listen to others share their experiences, and to do the assigned work so that she could have her turn to share.

Students' increased interest in and perception of mathematics permeating their everyday lives came from sharing their particular personal mathematics stories with their classmates and with their teacher and having those experiences valued in school. Students felt they added something valuable to mathematics classes and felt heard by fellow students and teachers.

HOW TEACHERS INCLUDED PERSONAL EXPERIENCES
IN MATHEMATICS

Over the past 6 years, I have worked with teachers who are including students' personal, out-of-school experiences in their classroom lessons. The following quote is typical of the emotionally engaged students I hear in these classrooms: "OOOOH. Oh, let me share mine! I get it! Oh, wait 'til you hear mine!"

The following are ways that teachers have effectively incorporated students' personal, out-of-school math problems into classroom math lessons. Even though these techniques were used for a number of math units at a number of grade levels, for consistency I'll limit the examples to those from units on money in elementary school.

Introducing a Math Concept

To introduce a math concept, a teacher can ask a leading question to solicit examples from students. For example, a teacher introducing counting money by fives or tens could ask the class a leading question: "Has anyone bought something that cost five or ten cents each?" "What was it and how many did you buy?"

Collecting Math Examples from the Neighborhood

For older students, teachers can teach the students to be anthropologists who record instances of using math outside school. For younger students, it helps to involve elders in this collecting. One teacher sent Neighborhood Link sheets home for her second-grade students to work on with an adult or older child to record out-of-school math experiences for the math being studied in school. At the top of the Neighborhood Link page for money was this text:

> Work with someone out of school. This can be a parent, grandparent, aunt, uncle, brother, sister, cousin, or other adult. Talk with this person about when you used money. Write one example of a time you used money. Give lots of details. You may draw a picture too. Later, in school, we will use this information to write a math problem.[1]

A second grader wrote, "I wanted to buy some candy. The candy is 50 cents. I had 25 cents. I got more. Now I have 50 cents." When the students returned their Links, their teacher introduced subsequent lessons using their examples. In this case, the teacher introduced the concept of "counting up" in money as an alternative to the computational approach of subtracting to find the unknown addend.

Journals

During language arts, daily journal entries sometimes focused on mathematics experiences the students had outside school. The children wrote their entries, drew accompanying pictures, and then two or three shared their work. When the class was studying money, the teacher asked students to write about a time they went to the store to buy something. One student wrote:

> I saw my friend at the store and she gave me a dollar for free. So when me and my grandfather were paying for the groceries, I bought M & Ms with my dollar. So the lady gave me a quarter and a dime, and that adds up to 35 cents.

Another student wrote:

> I made five dollars because I helped my next door neighbor clean up some leaves off of her flowers and then there was some more on the other side of the house and I got those leaves up and I made two more dollars and I went to the store and bought four bags of chips for a dollar.

This story has several math problems that a teacher could use in lessons on money, including how many dollars the student earned, how much money was left after spending the dollar, and how much a bag of chips cost.

Sometimes students' journals serve as valuable diagnostic tools by letting a teacher see what is understood and what is not by individual students. One student wrote, "I have four quarters and another set of four quarters and [so I] have two dollars." The illustration, however, showed a bill with five cents on it.

Writing Word Problems

A group of fifth graders who were struggling with solving word problems took their teacher's challenge and turned their journal stories into word problems for the rest of the class to solve. This turned out to be the most exciting use of personal math experiences for these students, who reveled in being able to solve classmate's problems instead of always having to solve the textbook problems. During these lessons, I documented a noticeable increase in students' engagement in solving problems. When the teacher put a classmates' problem on the overhead for everyone to solve, nearly all students worked on the problem and discussed it. When the teacher put a textbook problem on the overhead, less than half of the students even tried to solve the problem, even though text problems were generally much easier as judged by the number of steps involved in solving them, compared with the students' problems. Following are some of the problems written by these fifth graders.

> I had $204.00. I spent $65 on sneakers. Then I spent $30 more on my nails. Then I spent $9.00 more dollars on a shirt. For a moment, I thought I'd lost all my money. Then I said, "Oh, God, help me find my money." Finally I found my money. Then I kept on shopping in the mall. How much money do I have left if I also have to pay my rent? My rent money is $100.00.

This problem resulted in quite an animated discussion of different rents in the city. The teacher discovered that these fifth graders knew how much their families paid for rent, where rents were higher and lower, and some of the reasons why.

> I went to the store and bought 20 pieces of candy for 5 cents each and I bought 20 more pieces of candy for 5 cents each. How much did I spend?

> I work with my uncle at the pawn shop. I sell Playstation games there. I work there for a good reason and I get a good deal. I get paid $10 in two days. How much do I get paid in a day?

One day I went to the store. I had 5 dollars. I bought two packs of cookies. They each cost 25 cents. Then after that my sister asked me if she could have a dollar. I said yes. How much money do I have left? And how much money did I spend?

Lessons

Once students are writing their personal mathematics experiences, a teacher has a wealth of examples to use in lessons. Sometimes these problems are used as the introduction, or final example, in a lesson. At other times, the problems can be used when a teacher feels students are not grasping a concept. At that time, students' problems are used on the spur of the moment to reinforce and help students remember the concept. At still other times, students' problems can be used to add interest and immediate meaningfulness to a lesson. When students' attention is lagging, putting a student's problem before the class helps everyone focus and find similar problems in their journals or records. Just as audience is a powerful motivator for language arts writing, so is having the chance to share a math problem with classmates during a math lesson.

A second-grade student wrote in her journal, "I wanted to buy some candy. The candy is 50 cents. I had 25 cents. I got one more and now I have 50 cents." A problem that the teacher could pose to the class is, "What was the coin she got?"

Review

For review of a unit, teachers can give students several classmates' problems to solve, or ask the students to do another Neighborhood Link or journal entry. Often the second or third Neighborhood Link or journal entry will be more sophisticated and complete than the earlier ones, showing the increased understanding of the mathematics involved in the personal experiences. Students in one classroom also can create problems for students in other classrooms to solve, thereby extending community beyond the classroom.

HOW TEACHERS CHANGED

Nurturing the social and emotional aspects of students during mathematics classes changes teachers. It changes their understanding of what it means to include students' families and what it means to teach mathematics well to all students. Instead of viewing families as important only in parent–

teacher conferences and in helping with homework, teachers learn to recognize the involvement of the family and larger community in a student's learning and to find effective ways to tap into that involvement.

The power structure of the classroom changes when students' personal experiences are infused into mathematics lessons. No longer is the teacher the possessor of all knowledge and answers in the classroom. Who has the answers, who has the questions, who has the knowledge, all shift from the teacher as sole possessor to one of more equality. This involves a different power balance in the classroom, as well as a different conception of learning. No longer do students learn only what is in the teacher's head or the textbook, but students also learn from each other, from the challenge of learning to recognize problems in their life, and from reflecting on problems in their lives.[2]

By using students' outside experiences as springboards for mathematics lessons, teachers celebrate the worth of students' lives and what they have to offer in the classroom. The classroom becomes a community of learners and teachers. Both learn from each other and teach each other. What is learned is not only the traditional academic knowledge, but also social and emotional lessons.

IMPLICATIONS FOR TEACHER EDUCATION

As Zeuli and Ben-Avie (Chapter 2, this volume) and Pettigrew and Dolan (Chapter 7) contend, teachers must be taught and supported in teaching mathematics and science in ways that will ensure that all students succeed. Ladson-Billings's concern (noted at the beginning of this chapter) that schools of education are still teaching for idealized school populations rather than the needs of the students who are actually in schools today reminds us that schools of education must examine and often alter radically their preservice and continuing education courses to address these needs. What would this look like? While few schools of education can be used as models, some show glimpses of what is possible and desirable. The following is what I envision it will take for teacher education to more effectively address teacher preparation for the social/emotional and academic needs of today's diverse students, and includes what some schools of education are now doing.

Professors, students, teachers, parents, principals, school administrators, and community members must work closely together, so much so that education courses will be located in schools and in community centers, as well as in schools of education. Collaboration will be the norm, not an exception. To model how we want teachers to teach in schools, nearly all education courses will be collaboratively taught and will be as inquiry- and personally based as possible. Teamed professors will both teach simultaneously rather than in tag-team fashion and be specifically chosen for their differing expertise and views on a subject so that class discussions will be rich and challenging. For instance, a professor of school counseling might be paired with a professor of elementary mathematics, or a practicing high school teacher might be paired with a professor of philosophy of education. Team members will rotate so that professors get to know many different disciplines and viewpoints.

No longer will an individual classroom be the only locus of collaboration; rather, teachers and teacher educators from different sites will contribute to course sessions. Japan is using a collaborative model for lesson development. Teacher educators could include this with the pioneering work of the University of Virginia's CaseNex[3] for technology in teacher education courses, to use technology to enhance cross-site collaboration and courses. Not only would this add breadth to a course by having professors (and students) from very different settings contributing their perspectives, but it also could make team-taught classes financially feasible. While each institution has to pay for only one professor, each class is collaboratively taught, via telecommunications, by two or more professors from different institutions.

Education courses will be inquiry-based, with differentiation the norm rather than an exception. In essence, education courses will be taking the best of what special education sometimes has done—teaching collaboratively and tailoring a course so that every student can succeed. Rather than teaching in a lecture format and wasting the input of the second professor while only one is lecturing, courses will be more learner-centered, including discussions, small-group work, individual work, and workshops, while employing a variety of delivery modes. Courses will be integrally linked with field work in K–12 classrooms throughout the entire teacher education program so that class discussions and assignments will naturally include experiences in the classrooms as well as texts. Assignments will tap into teacher education students' personal interests and experiences as a way to be sure courses are relevant to each student, as well as to help students learn to synthesize prior experiences with new course content and to enrich discussions among class members. This will model how we want these future teachers to later teach their own students. Courses will be demanding, and schools of education will demand that all those entering teaching meet high standards. Those standards will include a high level of mastery of mathematics and science for elementary teachers, not just for specialists at higher grade levels.

As Pettigrew and Dolan (Chapter 7, this volume) argue, schools of education cannot expect to do this work alone; they must align with school districts and ideally with the corporate world (Fowler, Chapter 9, this volume). Inservice teacher education must be ongoing, providing support for teachers throughout their careers, and allowing teachers to learn from each other as well as from professors and specialists. Ideally, I would follow teacher education courses with seminars during student teaching and with study groups for full-time teachers in order to provide the ongoing support that I see necessary for sustaining teachers' growth. States will need to reassess how schools are funded. The current glaring inequities of funding perpetuate the high turnover of teachers in high-need districts, especially urban districts. Instead, if states refocus to put the best teachers and most funding in the highest-need schools, our society may begin to solve some larger societal problems. School counselors and psychologists will be integrally involved in helping empower all teachers, parents, and students to attend to social and emotional needs, with a clear message that students' social and emotional development is addressed not only by specialists or only in separate time slots but even in mathematics and science classes.

Teacher educators and student teachers will consult parents of K–12 students for their ideas on what is good for their children, and hence what future teachers need to know and be able to do. Students' personal experiences and concerns will be an integral part of both K–12 classrooms in which the student teachers work and teacher education classrooms. When relationships are considered as much as academic knowledge, then all of our students, kindergartners through teacher education students, will learn well.

NOTES

1. Thanks to Susan Hall, a graduate research assistant, for the conception and wording of the Neighborhood Link.

2. See Ensign (2001) for a fuller discussion of these power relationships in math classes.

3. University of Virginia's CaseNex (http://www.casenex.org) uses online multimedia cases to bring together preservice and inservice teachers to analyze educational problems and to create action plans to ensure student and school success. CaseNex students attend class sessions at their school site where an on-site instructor guides student work, which is a combination of classroom discussion and instruction, and distance discussions and instruction via the World Wide Web. Each case study focuses on a problem situation in a K–12 school. Through listserv discussions, chat discussions, and guest speakers who address questions from participants via streaming video, participants from very diverse areas of the world are

able to discuss educational problems. As of 2001, participants have been from 40 institutions of higher learning and public schools in the United States, Canada, Norway, England, and France.

REFERENCES

Ben-Avie, M. (2001, April). *The impact of a school-based academic and counseling intervention on the lifepaths of youth*. Paper presented at the annual meeting of the American Educational Research Association, Seattle.

Cochran-Smith, M. (2000). *The outcomes question in teacher education*. Vice-presidential address presented at the annual meeting of the American Educational Research Association, New Orleans.

Dewey, J. (1900). *The school and society*. New York: McClure, Philips.

Dewey, J. (1916). *Democracy and education*. New York: Free Press.

Ensign, J. (1997). Ritualizing sacredness in math, profaneness in language arts and social studies. *The Urban Review, 29*(4), 253–261.

Ensign, J. (2001, Spring). Culturally connected math problems in an urban school. *The Connecticut Mathematics Journal*, pp. 3–8.

Freire, P. (1993). *Pedagogy of the city* (D. Macedo, Trans.). New York: Continuum Press.

Ladson-Billings, G. (1992). Reading between the lines and beyond the pages: A culturally relevant approach to literacy teaching. *Theory into Practice, 31*(4), 312–320.

Noddings, N. (1992). *The challenge to care in schools*. New York: Teachers College Press.

Peterson, P. L. (1994). Knowledge transforming: Teachers, students, and researchers as learners in community. In J. Mangieri & C. C. Block (Eds.), *Creating powerful thinking in teachers and students: Diverse perspectives* (pp. 51–79). Fort Worth, TX: Harcourt Brace.

Stigler, J. W., & Hiebert, J. (1999). *The teaching gap: Best ideas from the world's teachers for improving education in the classroom*. New York: Free Press.

CHAPTER 7

Excellence and Equity: A Regional Consortium for Reforming Science Education

David Pettigrew & James Dolan

THIS CHAPTER DISCUSSES A PARTICULAR INSTANCE of systemic reform in science education aligned with the *National Science Education Standards* (NSES) as well as with the National Science Resources Center (NSRC) framework for systemic reform.[1] The reform in question involved Southern Connecticut State University and four school districts: New Haven, Hamden, North Branford, and Wallingford Public Schools. The collaborators forged a consensus about the essential reform documents and built a regional consortium. The project involved the selection and implementation of inquiry-centered, Standards-aligned science materials, including "Science and Technology for Children" and "Full Option Science System" kits[2]; intensive and sustained professional development; and the establishment of a centralized kit-materials support center. This chapter offers our account of educational change as a result of implementing the Standards.

Such accounts of local experiences are crucial for the sustainability of systemic reform. While a theoretical framework has been set forth in the above-referenced reform documents, the implementation of the Standards and the Standards-aligned science kits presents curriculum supervisors and their school districts with enormous challenges. Educators need to make use of experiences of other school districts and counties as they determine how to implement Standards-aligned reform in their own districts.

Experience across the country shows that all the components of systemic reform are equally important for success. Standards-aligned reform presents daunting challenges because the principles of systemic reform and equity demand that the science kits be provided for all children of all teachers in all of a district's classrooms. Providing a few kits to a few interested or motivated teachers is not systemic reform. The necessity of district-wide saturation, so to speak, implies critical organizational considerations. On the one hand, placing a science kit in a classroom is pointless unless the teacher receives adequate professional development.[3] On the other hand, it is highly unlikely that a school district could afford or manage to implement the science kits without a centralized kit-materials resource center. Such a center provides for low-cost replenishments and multiple uses of the same kit each year in the school district. Thus, all the components of systemic reform must work in concert to bring Standards-aligned science to the classroom.

This crisis of educational preparedness with respect to excellence and equity in science education is complex. Yet, one theme that resurfaces constantly is that of a time crisis—the lack of commitment to spending time on science education as well as the misuse of time for science in the educational day. One of the first challenges for reform in inquiry-centered science education is to provide a place, in the sense of adequate time, for inquiry-centered science activities during the school day.

A CRISIS OF TIME AND VISION

Indeed, numerous recent reports and studies, including, for example, *Prisoners of Time: Report of the National Education Commission on Time and Learning* (1994) and the *A Splintered Vision: An Investigation of US Science and Mathematics Education* (Schmidt, McKnight, & Raizin, 1997), provide disturbing observations. They argue, first, that grossly inadequate time is granted to mathematics and science education in the general curriculum; and second, that when science education does hold a place in the curriculum, the time actually spent on the subject is wasted on unproductive or even counterproductive exercises. A fundamental insight of the Standards is that authentic inquiry-centered science activities in the classroom require periods of time of an extended duration.

The Connecticut Academy for Education in Mathematics, Science, & Technology issued a 1995 report entitled "The Case for More Time and the Better Use of Time in Connecticut's Schools." This academy is a nonprofit corporation designated by the legislature to act as the broker and advocate for high standards in the teaching and learning of mathematics, science, and technology for all citizens. In the report, the academy states that our children have 6 to 8 fewer weeks of schooling than their peers in other leading industrial countries and spend less time on core subjects, including mathematics, science, and technology. In this regard, our educational system is not addressing the rapidly changing demands of our society. Further, in addition to the lack of time devoted to mathematics and science education, the report speaks of the dislocation and disjunction of time in our educational institutions. Through the standard 50-minute class, the 6-hour school day, and the 10-month school year, we are compartmentalized by a calculus of time frames and unyielding schedules. As the National Education Commission on Time and Learning (1994) asserts, "We are prisoners of time, captives of the school clock and calendar" (p. 4).

These indictments of an education system that suffers from dislocation, disjunction, and fragmentation in science education (a crisis in what we might refer to as the time economy of our nation's classrooms) are echoed in *A Splintered Vision*, which charges that, lacking national leadership, U.S. mathematics and science education suffers from a piecemeal, chaotic curriculum—splintered visions. These splintered visions produce unfocused curricula and textbooks that fail to define clearly what is intended to be taught. They influence teachers to implement diffuse learning goals in their classrooms. They emphasize familiarity with many topics rather than concentrated attention to a few. And they likely lower the academic performance of students who spend years in such a learning environment. Our curricula, textbooks, and teaching all are "a mile wide and an inch deep" (Schmidt et al., 1997, p. 62).

U.S. textbooks cover too many topics—as many as 45 separate topics in an eighth-grade math class in comparison to Japanese or German texts that cover only four or five basic areas. The lack of a focused curriculum has a negative impact on instruction. U.S. teachers predictably rush to cover the textbook topics and fail to spend sufficient time on any one topic (Schmidt et al., 1997). Mathematics and science textbooks are so splintered and episodic that teachers are often unable to connect topics from chapter to chapter or within the same academic year. Additionally, the fragmentation minimizes the possibility that teachers from different disciplines will be able to make meaningful connections between and among their subject matter areas. The exposure to science that results from such fragmentation has been compared to watching television facilitated by remote control devices—channel surfing. Further, such a disconnected array of topics to be covered makes effective professional development activities for teachers almost impossible. This pronounced lack of curricular coherence bespeaks a lack of vision on the national level. The authors of *A Splintered Vision* proclaim that "no one is at the helm" (Schmidt et al., 1997, p. 1).

The *National Science Education Standards* were precisely an attempt to fill this leadership vacuum. One of the most significant aspects of the Standards, in the context of their comprehensive vision for excellence, is their focus on the need for more extended time for science in the curriculum. The NSES call for more time for science education in order to accommodate the demands of an active, collaborative, inquiry-based learning environment. The Standards assert, moreover, that science education requires time to develop a learning community and time to instill a commitment to learning: Both are fundamental to the educational process. The NSES describe the obvious need for time for students to "try out ideas, to make mistakes, to ponder, and to discuss with one another" (National Research Council, 1996, p. 44). With time for extended inquiry comes the possibility of collaboration and communication. The Standards emphasize that "science is often a collaborative endeavor, and all science depends on the ultimate sharing and debating of ideas" (National Research Council, 1996, p. 32). The focus of the NSES on the need for time for science, then, is central to their vision of excellence as a collaborative process of inquiry and discovery.[4] In addition, the Standards link the issue of time to equity. Providing adequate time for scientific inquiry allows the teacher to give proper attention to inclusion of

> those who traditionally have not received encouragement and opportunity to pursue science—women and girls, students of color, students with disabilities, and students with limited English proficiency. It implies attention to various styles of learning, adaptations to meet the needs of special students and differing sources of motivation. (National Research Council, 1996, p. 221)

A VISION OF EXCELLENCE AND EQUITY

It is perhaps unexpected that a document such as the *National Science Education Standards* would be conceived by the National Research Council; unexpected that such an august group of research scientists would oversee the development of a document as pedagogically progressive as the Standards. Indeed, this text could be said to relegate textbook-based science to the recycling bin. Our examination of science textbooks confirms that they are full of content errors. The Standards de-emphasize learning a text-bound vocabulary of science and put new emphasis on science as process. The process is designed to facilitate inferences on the part of students. The teacher is no longer the repository of knowledge, but rather a facilitator and a collaborator. The Standards call for teachers to "encourage and model the skills of scientific inquiry, as well as the curiosity, openness to new ideas, and skepticism, that characterize science" (National Research Council, 1996, p. 37).

These suggestions echo those of an earlier National Council of Teachers of Mathematics (NCTM) text that asserts that mathematics must be seen as "an activity and a process, not simply as a body of content to be mastered. Throughout, there is an emphasis on doing mathematics, recognizing connections, and valuing the enterprise" (NCTM, 1995, p. vi). This perspective brings current algebra pedagogy in many institutions into an immediate dilemma: Existing courses are designed to cover vast quantities of material, while the learning style promoted by the NCTM Standards requires the time for in-depth, hands-on, inquiry-based, collaborative exploration of a smaller number of integrated topics and themes.

Indeed, the first step for a Standards-aligned science class is the development of a community of learners and the modeling of the skills of scientific inquiry (National Research Council, 1996). The teacher needs to have the students operate as an inclusive group with a shared mission. The emphasis here is on working together rather than in isolation—pairs reporting to groups, groups reporting to the class as a whole, and the teacher serving as stimulus and facilitator. The process of learning accommodates the broadest spectrum of learning styles. The teacher in a Standards-aligned classroom guides and facilitates the scientific inquiry of all students in a learning community. The teacher must respond to student diversity in the classroom and orchestrate participation for all members of the classroom. Such a classroom models the insistence of the Standards that science is a human endeavor involving "women and men of various social and ethnic backgrounds with diverse interests, talents, qualities, and motivations" (National Research Council, 1996, p. 170).

Moreover, rather than presenting science as an isolated discipline in a rarefied context, the Standards-aligned curriculum makes connections to the history of science and personal and social perspectives in the process of what can be referred to as the humanization of science. Rather than a pedagogy rigidly based on an eighteenth- or nineteenth-century view of the world concerned with taxonomic systems that segmented and compartmentalized the world, the NSES emphasize a fundamentally integrated mode of inquiry and an interdisciplinary nature of knowledge, stating that science needs to be connected to other school subjects (National Research Council, 1996). Such a connection is to be made particularly, the Standards assert, to mathematics. The emphasis in the NSES on the history of science and personal and social perspectives opens the way to a fuller appreciation of science as a human activity—one that implies responsibility to the human community.

The national vision offered by the NSES makes explicit the principle that educational excellence and equity are mutually interdependent:

> The intent of the Standards can be expressed in a single phrase: Science standards *for all students*. The phrase embodies both excellence and equity. The Standards apply to all students, regardless of age, gender, cultural or ethnic background, disabilities, aspirations or interest and motivation in science. (National Research Council, 1996, p. 2, emphasis added)

The mutual interdependence of excellence and equity give the Standards the potential to be a truly inclusive national vision. In our view, this point must never be forgotten and can never be overly emphasized. The Standards assert that it is exigent that students be given equitable opportunities to learn science: access to "skilled professional teachers, adequate classroom time, a rich array of learning materials, accommodating work spaces, and resources" (National Research Council, 1996, p. 2). The NSES assume that the inclusion of all students in challenging learning opportunities is absolutely crucial for the excellence of any science pedagogy. They emphatically reject any situation in science education where some people are discouraged from pursuing science and excluded from opportunities to learn science (National Research Council, 1996). The Standards state that the "equity principles must be incorporated into science education policies if the vision of the Standards is to be achieved" (National Research Council, 1996, p. 233).

Thus, the Standards respond to this crisis of equity by calling for a fundamental reorientation with respect to science pedagogy—for a pedagogy that provides both an innovative method of learning science and an equitable involvement for minority teachers and students. Perhaps it is not an accident that the themes of excellence and equity are inextricably linked in the pedagogy itself. Fundamental to the teaching and learning method that is essential to the Standards, are the themes of collaboration, inclusion, and respect for the diversity of ideas and contributions to the process of inquiry.

MOVING FROM THEORY TO PRACTICE: A MODEL FOR SYSTEMIC, STANDARDS-ALIGNED REFORM IN INQUIRY-CENTERED SCIENCE EDUCATION

Promising efforts at Standards-based reform are underway in various parts of the United States. The following section concerns our own experience with one such reform effort based at Southern Connecticut State University (SCSU) in New Haven. The story of change to be recounted as a critical model herein covers significant events spanning the period from 1993 through 2002. The effort led to a number of significant outcomes. The principal outcomes to be discussed include (1) the development of a working and evolving consensus concerning Standards-aligned systemic reform documents; (2) the selection and adoption of Standards-aligned, inquiry-centered science materials in four school districts; (3) the formation of a regional consortium for systemic reform involving SCSU, the New Haven, Hamden, North Branford, and Wallingford Public Schools, and Bayer Corporation; (4) the creation of an array of intensive and sustained inquiry-centered professional development activities for teachers; and (5) the establishment of a centralized science materials resource center.

Nurturing a Consensus for Standards-Aligned Reform

The abovementioned developments emerged from a collaboration between Southern Connecticut State University and the school districts. While the consortium was formed in September 1999, the collaboration that led to it began in 1992. It is important to note that the development of a consensus for change required a patient, concerted effort over the course of approximately 7 years. Initially, the collaboration was formed between SCSU and the New Haven Public Schools. As one of the oldest and largest teacher preparation programs in the region, SCSU maintains numerous programs with school districts in the state. The collaboration devoted to science education partakes of this tradition.

The early stages of the collaboration between SCSU and the New Haven Public Schools were undertaken with the support of Project CONNSTRUCT, a program of Connecticut's National Science Foundation Statewide Systemic Initiative under the auspices of the Connecticut Academy for Education in Mathematics, Science, & Technology. From 1993 to 1995, university faculty and New Haven teachers and administrators engaged in a number of open-ended discussions and collaborative projects. The discussions were designed first to build trust and communication between university faculty and public school teachers, and second to identify strengths and weaknesses of educational practices at the university and in the public schools. These dialogues helped develop an appreciation and consensus for the emerging curriculum standards in mathematics and science. In addition, the discussions led to collaborative projects, including "Co-Teaching Collaborations," as part of which SCSU faculty and New Haven teachers would co-teach a range of courses required for mathematics and science teacher certification.[5] The presence of the public school teacher in the university teacher preparation class was invaluable. SCSU college students in these courses undertook mentoring opportunities in the New Haven Public Schools, as part of which they engaged in hands-on learning activities with New Haven schoolchildren. New Haven Public School classes, in turn, visited SCSU for hands-on mathematics manipulatives workshops, with SCSU students in attendance. SCSU faculty and New Haven teachers participated in Project CONNSTRUCT "Workshops for Restructuring," experiencing and discussing the virtues of hands-on, inquiry-based learning activities.

As a result of these 3½ years of collaborative reform activities, faculty at the university and the public schools achieved a new level of cooperation and mutual appreciation for their respective challenges and initiatives. University and public school faculty operated in the dialogues and interactions as peers with knowledge and experience of equal merit.[6] Administrators at each of the institutions were similarly involved in important communication and collaborative decisions regarding reform efforts, as well as the financial support that those efforts required.

Building on this important background, a "Science Education Dialogue" was formed in September 1995—again, with support from Project CONNSTRUCT—to undertake a careful review of the *National Science Education Standards* (then in draft form). The first key element in the process of science education reform was to begin to reach a grass-roots consensus about the reform documents and the priority of inquiry-centered learning. The importance of developing an atmosphere of trust and collegiality conducive to systemic reform involving institutions of higher education and the public schools must not be underestimated.

Selecting Inquiry-Centered Science Curriculum Materials

Another key element of our efforts involved the identification of Standards-aligned science materials. At that time, in 1995, a number of science kit curricula were becoming available to teachers: "Science and Technology for Children" (STC) and "Full Option Science System" (FOSS) kits. The STC and FOSS kits were designed by experienced teachers together with distinguished scientists and engineers in the context of the *National Science Education Standards* to usher in a new era of equity in elementary science education in the United States. They were field tested in urban centers with high percentages of schoolchildren from ethnic groups that are traditionally underserved and underrepresented in the fields of mathematics, science, and technology. The first page of each STC teacher's guide, for example, documents the sites of the extensive field testing of the STC kits across the United States, including Washington, DC.

The STC and FOSS kits are designed to contain nearly all the science materials needed for up to 12 weeks of hands-on, inquiry-centered activities for a classroom. A teacher's guide and student activity books for each kit enable a teacher to organize a cumulative set of increasingly complex and challenging age-appropriate activities for the children over the course of the unit. The STC and FOSS kits transform the classroom, engendering an engagement and excitement that spread to other subjects. The kits link science activities to reading, writing, history, mathematics, art, and other disciplines. The inquiry-centered pedagogy launches fresh investigations in other disciplines.

Our science education dialogue, then, focused on the STC and FOSS kits. The discussions benefited at this stage (as well as at every other stage of the reform process) from the presence and experience of the elementary school teachers who had already attempted to implement inquiry-centered learning methods in their classrooms.

Intensive and Sustained Professional Development in Inquiry-Centered Science

Having begun to reach a consensus with respect to the Standards, and having identified the science materials, we rapidly recognized the need for intensive and sustained professional development in order to allow teachers to begin to use the kits in their classrooms. Beginning in 1996, we designed and implemented the first of five sessions of a successful Standards-aligned graduate course at SCSU funded by grants from the Connecticut Department of Higher Education Dwight D. Eisenhower Professional Development Program. The intensive summer graduate course at SCSU (approximately 80 hours each summer) trained leader master-teachers—kit experts (first in New Haven and then in Hamden, North Branford, and Wallingford). The innovative graduate course immerses the teachers in the science activities contained in the STC and FOSS kits.

The basic structure of the graduate course has remained the same since its inception. Teams of teachers from each of the four school districts participate in the course. As the course has evolved, one section, for example, in 2001, focused on grades K–4 and a second section focused on grades 5–8. The course meets 4 hours a day, 4 days a week, for 5 weeks beginning in July. This is roughly equivalent to meeting for 6 lab hours a week over a regular 15-week semester.

This intensive schedule allows for the primary value of the course: the guided immersion of the teachers in experience with the authentic science activities that are contained in the science kits. The schedule allows for real-time pacing of the science activities as they are sequenced in the STC and FOSS teacher's guides and student activity books. The teachers experience the kits as they themselves will in turn facilitate those activities for the children in their classrooms. The course has been designed to exemplify a Standards-based classroom and to enable participants to develop Standards-based classrooms in their own educational environments.

Course participants carry out a representative set of hands-on, inquiry-based investigations appropriate to an effective science curriculum. The teachers see how the kits for their own grades are related to kits for earlier and later grades. The course develops participants' knowledge of the life, earth, and physical sciences. Providing extensive experience with exemplary teaching and learning materials, the course emphasizes a critical combination of conceptual understanding and operational performance. The selected units have been designed to provide experiences that are appropriate to the cognitive development of children at the designated grade levels for each unit. The entire course is lab-based, with no formal lectures. Teachers receive three graduate credits and/or the equivalent in CEUs.

A number of examples of teacher experiences with the kits can be summarized briefly here. For example, during our 5-week course, teachers are able to carry out many of the activities in the STC third-grade "Plant Growth and Development" kit. The kit involves bean plants that grow quickly enough to allow students to measure, study, graph, and draw the complete growth cycle over the course of 8 weeks. The STC fourth-grade "Motion and Design" kit involves teachers in constructing and competing with scale-model plastic vehicles powered by rubber bands. The "Motion and Design" kit, as in the case of many of the STC and FOSS kits, entails working with a partner, requires careful attention to detail, and involves prediction, measurement, and data collection. The sixth-grade "Measuring Time" kit, in common with many other STC kits, offers a Spanish-language edition of the written materials. With the "Measuring Time" kit, the teachers perform experiments, for example, with a pendulum. Then, on the basis of the experimental understanding that they gain, they construct a functioning escapement clock with materials provided in the kit.

The science kits are designed to encourage collaborative inquiry in place of textbooks and lectures. The teacher-participants in the summer graduate course work through the student activity books as their students will. The teacher's guides and student activity books are designed to sequence lessons so that the students make inferences gradually as activities increase in complexity.

The graduate course has been taught collaboratively by SCSU Physics Professor and Chair James Dolan, Ph.D., along with co-teachers from the elementary schools. Both of the co-teachers have implemented the STC kits in their own classrooms. In 1996, the course was co-taught by Margaret Andrews, an elementary school teacher at New Haven's Helene Grant Elementary School. In 1997 and 1998, the course was co-taught by Elizabeth Doherty, then a teacher at New Haven's Vincent Mauro Elementary School. In 1999, we held a course devoted to middle school mathematics. In 2000, Ms. Doherty co-taught a section of the course devoted to grades 5–8, and the K–4 section of the course was co-taught by Jeanne Kim Baldwin, a teacher at New Haven's Edgewood Elementary School.

This decidedly collaborative model for professional development is a direct response to the call to action set forth in the Standards for hands-on, inquiry-based learning. As the Standards indicate, "The current reform effort in science education requires a substantive change in how science is taught. Implicit in this reform is an equally substantive change in professional development practices at all levels" (National Research Council, 1996, p. 56). SCSU and the New Haven Public Schools sought to develop a Standards-based graduate course providing a timely response to the professional development needs raised by the Standards. The model course was designed to follow the Standards to "engage . . . practicing teachers in active learning that builds their knowledge, understanding, and ability" (National Research Council, 1996, p. 56).

The intensive graduate course sessions offered in 1996, 1997, 1998, and 2000 have produced a cadre of leader master-teachers. In 1998, following the graduate course and with the support of Bayer Corporation, New Haven's Science Curriculum Supervisor, Dr. Marc Blosveren, made the decision to implement the STC and FOSS kits as New Haven's official science curriculum.[7] Following the graduate course in July 2000, Hamden and North Branford Public Schools also resolved to implement the kits in their classrooms.

The leader master-teachers who were trained during the intensive summer course played the crucial role of leading professional development workshops for teachers from the participating school districts. While the graduate course now serves 30 teachers each summer, the workshops led by the leader master-teachers train hundreds of teachers from the school districts in 10-hour workshops held in the fall, spring, and summer. Since 1998, the leader master-teachers have trained approximately 500 teachers, many on multiple kits.

A Centralized Science Materials Resource Center

An indispensable element of systemic reform involves the establishment of a centralized kit-materials resource center for kit refurbishment, ensuring the low-cost replenishment and reuse of kits for years to come. The National Science Resource Center (1997) asserts, "Experience has shown that science will be taught more effectively if science materials are managed by the school district and made available to teachers when they need them. The most effective way for a school district to do this is to create a science materials resource center" (p. 90). Moreover, the national model for a science materials resource center that we have followed is one that provides science materials to multiple school districts. The centralized materials resource center provides for the efficient and cost-effective distribution of the kits to increasing numbers of classroom teachers in a growing number of school districts.

A Standards-aligned pedagogy expects that all teachers will receive the necessary and sustained professional development, and that all classrooms will receive the science materials. The centralized materials resource center is the only way to guarantee the achievement of our goal of equity: providing world-class science materials to all our children.

Accordingly, throughout the 1999–2000 school year, our consortium discussed the need to establish a materials resource center. After a year of considering possible locations for preparation for the September 1, 2000, delivery of kits, SCSU invited the consortium to establish an 1,800-square-foot science materials resource center on its campus. The science materials resource center houses the science kits for the school districts. A small staff prepares them for delivery to the classrooms, and then retrieves and refurbishes the kits for up to two additional classroom uses during the year. Between September 2000 and March 2001, the center made approximately 750 kit deliveries to the consortium's school districts. In the initial stages, the center delivered two different kits in the course of the year to participating teachers. Our goal is to reach a point where we can deliver three different kits a year to participating teachers. Districts need to recognize that centralized materials resource centers are not extraneous to systemic reform but rather are one of the pillars of a successful project.

PROMISE FOR THE FUTURE: CHALLENGES YET TO COME

Significant challenges remain in our efforts to promote systemic reform. For example, the consortium needs to turn its attention to yet another component of the NSRC's paradigm for systemic reform: assessing inquiry-centered student learning on the one hand and assessing the science program on the other hand. The National Science Resource Center (1997) asserts, for example, that "traditional tests—usually multiple-choice, short-answer tests given at the end of a unit of study—cannot assess all the richness of learning that takes place in the inquiry-centered science classroom" (p. 100). The implementation of inquiry-centered pedagogy requires the implementation of more appropriate methods of assessment, such as embedded assessments that are "woven, or embedded, into the instructional sequence of the module . . . part of the activities that naturally occur in a lesson" (p. 103). The STC and FOSS teacher's guides contain suggestions for such assessments that view instruction and assessment as inextricably interwoven. Teachers in the four school districts are gaining experience with student portfolios that manifest the flow of learning. The consortium plans to gather the experiences of the teachers and address assessment in the near future. In the interest of equity, we hope to replicate our project for systemic reform statewide in Connecticut.

Each of these challenges that have just been identified were addressed, in part, by a new advanced graduate course during the summer of 2001. Southern Connecticut State University received a Department of Higher Education Eisenhower Professional Development grant for the purpose of refining and nurturing a more comprehensive vision for a professional development plan with statewide applicability. The professional development scheme that we envision has three levels.

Level One professional development involves the 5- to 10-hour workshops on using kits at the teacher's grade level, in the individual districts, at their own facilities. The idea is for all teachers to be able to take these workshops. The same workshops are repeated each year, to cover new hires and teachers who switched grade levels. Therefore teachers who stayed at the same grade level would be trained only the first year they were using that kit. (This level is "nuts and bolts" training on the kits—extremely important for novices, but we know that we need to provide follow-up workshops in the future, since 10 hours of training is not nearly enough by itself.) Most of these Level One workshops are presented by teachers who were trained in the summer graduate course at SCSU under the Eisenhower grants. The Level One workshops introduce teachers to the contents of the kits and selected lessons or activities. Although Professors Dolan and Pettigrew initially designed and coordinated these workshops, the school districts have assumed the role of providing them.

Level Two professional development involves the summer graduate courses (discussed above) that provide extensive and sustained immersion in experience with the kits. Level Two professional development produces kit experts, or leader master-teachers, who are indispensable for systemic reform. On the one hand, the 5-week graduate course produces leader master-teachers because of the extended time format. On the other hand, the course is effective because teachers work with kits spanning a number of grade levels and discern the connections and conceptual developments from grade to grade.

The Eisenhower grant received for summer 2001 supported an advanced course for those already trained at Level Two. Teachers who had already completed Level Two professional development had the chance to advance to a deeper understanding of inquiry-based learning. The participants in the advanced graduate course, along with SCSU professors, reviewed and refined the best practices in the professional development activities being pursued by our regional consortium. The course participants discussed ideas for a new Standards-aligned graduate degree program in inquiry-centered science education at SCSU. The development of a graduate program in inquiry-centered science would constitute "Level Three" of our professional development vision. The course immersed the teachers in action research and reflection, engaging practical and theoretical themes that are crucial for the development of a comprehensive vision for Standards-aligned systemic reform.

As part of our efforts to continuously improve science education, we invited Dr. Michael Klentschy, Superintendent of Schools in El Centro, California, to give a presentation to our teacher-participants in the 2001 summer graduate course. Dr. Klentschy implemented the science kits in his school district over the past 5 years. He adhered to the NSRC recommendations and provided each teacher with 20 hours of professional development each year. Teachers learned to facilitate the science activities in the kits and, more important, learned to use the science activities to generate language development and mathematical learning. Dr. Klentschy presented compelling, comprehensive, longitudinal data that show a striking correlation between inquiry-centered science learning and increases in student achievement in his school district. In fact, the science initiative was the only initiative introduced in the school district in the period in question. Moreover, over the course of the 5-year project the district (in which Spanish is the first language for more than 50% of the student population) recorded a 50% increase in student achievement on the California SAT 9 test.

Our initiative has undergone remarkable developments over the past 10 years and El Centro's story was particularly inspirational. Our 2001 summer graduate course participants identified specific areas that need to be addressed to improve our teaching and learning with the science kits. These include: (1) inquiry-centered learning—philosophical foundations as well as exploration of best practices; (2) assessment—research-based program assessment as well as embedded authentic assessment of student performance in inquiry-centered learning; (3) deepened appreciation of the science content implicit in the inquiry-based activities contained in the kits; (4) implications of the science kits for special education; (5) science and language development; and (6) science and mathematics.

FORGING A NATIONAL CONSENSUS

We conclude by taking issue with one perspective presented in *A Splintered Vision* (Schmidt et al., 1997). It reserves particularly severe language for its reference to the lack of focus in educational policy. In the early stages of our work it might have been our position that we would owe the Standards at least our tentative allegiance. We might have, as Gerald Holton (1978) put it, undertaken a "suspension of our disbelief" (p. 71) with respect to the Standards in the interest of a national vision that the text could engender. Now, we believe the Standards, along with the NSRC paradigm for systemic reform, have had the chance to emerge as nothing less than visionary documents that have had a practical impact on science education reform efforts in greater New Haven as they have across the United States.

Moreover, the different voices that have emerged in the past decade have not been as cacophonous as the executive summary of *A Splintered Vision* would have us believe. From the NCTM Standards and *Science for All Children*, to the *National Science Education Standards*, there have been fundamentally consistent and common themes. It has not escaped our attention that those themes—emphasizing experiential learning, encouraging teachers to become facilitators of inquiry, and education as a social and transformative process with vital appeal—have a formidable philosophical antecedent. These themes genuinely echo the educational philosophy of John Dewey (1938/1963), who believed that experiential learning is nothing if not social. The NSES and the NSRC's *Science for All Children*, thus, are not new but rather reaffirm and focus, with the guiding principles of excellence and equity, the destiny of Dewey's educational vision.

NOTES

1. The National Science Resources Center of the National Research Council is operated by the Smithsonian Institution and the National Academy of Sciences to improve the teaching of science in the nation's schools. The NSRC collects and disseminates information about exemplary teaching resources, develops and disseminates curriculum materials, and sponsors outreach activities, specifically in the areas of leadership development and technical assistance, to help school districts develop and sustain hands-on science programs.

2. "The Science and Technology for Children" units were developed by the National Science Resources Center and the Smithsonian Institution and are distributed by Carolina Biological Supply. "The Full Option Science System" kits were developed by the Lawrence Hall of Science and are distributed by Delta Education.

3. The definition of "adequate" professional development may vary from district to district, but ideally each teacher should receive 20 to 25 hours of professional development each year for 4 to 5 years. Over the course of the years, the teachers learn to facilitate the activities in the science kits for their classes, and also learn science content, inquiry-centered learning assessment, and other areas.

4. *Rallying the Whole Village: The Comer Process for Reforming Education*, edited by James P. Comer, Norris M. Haynes, Edward T. Joyner, and Michael Ben-Avie, 1996, provides a prescient outline for university–school partnerships as well as the improved use of instructional time in the school day.

5. The author of the conceptual architecture for the Connecticut Academy's Project CONNSTRUCT competitive grants was Robert Gelbach, Southern Connecticut State University professor of political science. When the grant was received, Connecticut established an independent administrative body called the Connecticut Academy for Education in Mathematics, Science, & Technology.

6. It was crucial for the project that senior SCSU faculty were involved in these innovative activities. In the early Project CONNSTRUCT "Dialogues," SCSU senior mathematics faculty participants included Professors Robert Washburn, Helen Bass, and Leo Kuczynski, and senior science faculty included Professors James Dolan (physics), William Condon (chemistry), James Fullmer (earth science), and Noble Proctor (biology). Their involvement provided important leadership for the project. Science education faculty included Professors Milford Deprey, Joel Meisel, and Susan Hageman. Gateway Community Technical College was represented by science professor Robert Tremblay.

Systemic reform efforts at SCSU benefited from support at all administrative levels. The Dean of Education, Dr. Rodney Lane, and the then Dean of Arts and Sciences, J. Philip Smith, along with the late Vice President for Academic Affairs Anthony Pinciaro, provided unqualified support of the project. SCSU President Michael J. Adanti also encouraged this project as well as many other creative collaborations with New Haven and area school districts.

7. Bayer Corporation has been recognized nationally for its commitment to systemic reform across the United States (see National Science Resource Center, 1997, pp. 129–130). The West Haven-based Pharmaceutical Division has provided crucial support for our project. In 1998, following meetings with Mr. Keith Kelley, Bayer contributed to the summer graduate course for New Haven teachers. In many crucial respects Bayer's support provided the necessary momentum to move our efforts at systemic reform to a new level. While their contribution initially purchased science kits for New Haven, a significant portion of the contribution was to fund the initial operating costs of the science materials resource center.

REFERENCES

Comer, J. P., Haynes, N. M., Joyner, E. T., & Ben-Avie, M. (Eds.). (1996). *Rallying the whole village: The Comer process for reforming education.* New York: Teachers College Press.

Connecticut Academy for Education in Mathematics, Science, and Technology. (1995). *The case for more time and the better use of time in Connecticut's schools,* Middletown: Author.

Dewey, J. (1963). *Education and experience.* New York: Collier Books. (Original work published 1938)

Holton, G. J. (1978). *The scientific imagination: Case studies.* Cambridge: Cambridge University Press.

National Council of Teachers of Mathematics. (1995). *Curriculum and evaluation standards for school mathematics: Addenda series, grades 9–12, algebra in a technological world.* Reston, VA: Author.

National Education Commission on Time and Learning. (1994). *Prisoners of time: Report of the National Education Commission on Time and Learning.* Washington, DC: Government Printing Office.

National Research Council. (1996). *National science education standards.* Washington, DC: National Academy Press.

National Science Resource Center. (1997). *Science for all children: A guide to improving elementary science education in your school district.* Washington, DC: National Academy Press.

Schmidt, W. H., McKnight, C. C. & Raizin, S. A. (Eds.). (1997). *A splintered vision: An investigation of US science and mathematics education.* Boston: Kluwer Academic.

CHAPTER 8

Stretching Students' Future Orientation

Mary L. Moran with Michael Ben-Avie

A GROUP OF STUDENTS who had been awarded a full college scholarship were not taking advantage of learning activities that would help prepare them for their future. A pivotal moment occurred during a math session that had been arranged for them at a university—the students' behavior undermined the attempts of the adults to forge a university partnership for them. Mary Moran, the coordinator, realized that the students first needed to learn how to set and accomplish goals. This chapter describes the goal-setting activities and outcomes of the Houston students in the 12-year ScholarshipBuilder Program, which ended in June 2000.

In the fall of 1988, 250 families received notification of an extraordinary opportunity: Their first-grade children had been selected at random to receive a full college scholarship from the philanthropic foundation of Merrill Lynch & Co., Inc. The families, in each of 10 densely populated American inner cities, were told that the Merrill Lynch Foundation had created a fund called the ScholarshipBuilder Program and that the Foundation would earmark as an obligation $2,000 per year per child for 12 years. By the year 2000 there would be sufficient funds to send each student to the college of his or her choice. They also were told that Merrill Lynch would be partnering with the National Urban League, the Urban League affiliate in their city, their city's school system, and their child's school to provide support services as needed.

After 12 years, it was clear that the ScholarshipBuilder students had defied the odds in terms of high school graduation. In November 2000, the national ScholarshipBuilder administration expected the students to achieve a graduation rate of 94% over a 3-year period. This graduation rate is in striking contrast to the rates of comparable inner-city schools. *High School Graduation Rates in the United States*, a report prepared at the Center for Civic Innovation at the Manhattan Institute (Greene, 2001), shows that "the national graduation rate for the class of 1998 was 74%. For White students the rate was 78%, while it was 56% for African American students and 54% for Latino students" (p. i). In Houston—where Mary Moran coordinated the ScholarshipBuilder Program—the graduation rate was 52%, whereas for Mary Moran's group it was 94%.

Overall, the ScholarshipBuilder Program demonstrated that a business/community organization project can have a lifelong impact on students' development and their families' future. Among the 10 ScholarshipBuilder cities, there was great variation in programming. All of the sites had positive outcomes for the local Merrill Lynch employees who mentored the students, the local branch of the National Urban League, and the students. When caring, qualified adults make deliberate preparations and appropriate and timely interventions, students will have significant and positive outcomes. In this chapter, the work of Mary Moran is highlighted because of the goal-setting program that was implemented in Houston. The following is a brief overview of what we learned about goal setting and its importance to social and emotional development as it relates to math and science learning (a full description appears in Ben-Avie, Steinfeld, & Vergnetti, 2000).

Adolescents often engage in magical thinking. They want to get from Point A to Point B, but even if they know how to get there, they may expect "something" to intervene and do the actual process for them. For example, many teenagers behave as if in some magic way college applications will fill themselves out and mail themselves by the correct deadline. In Houston, the students engaged in bimonthly goal-setting meetings—to learn how to set personal and educational goals. The Houston students learned to align their short-term goals with their long-term goals. This makes achieving goals real and possible. For example: If I want to become a doctor, that means that I have to achieve my weekly goal of passing the math test right now. If asked, "What could a school start doing tomorrow that would impact students' engagement in math and science learning?" one answer would be goal setting.

In the opening chapter of this volume (Ben-Avie et al.), we theorized that student engagement in math and science activities occurs in at least three ways: cognitively, behaviorally, and psychologically. Cognitive engagement refers to knowing and understanding. Behavioral engagement refers to how the teacher structures and presents the math and science activities and how the student is involved in the learning process. Psychological engagement refers to the emotional connection that the student makes with the teacher, the other students, the material being taught, and his or her developing sense of future orientation. Future orientation, as we explained in the opening chapter, is the ability to conceive of one's development. We found that the most important predictor of academic and professional competencies was future orientation. (Academic and professional competencies is the variable that measures the consistent demonstration of attributes, such as work ethic, that contribute to high academic achievement and that employers consider desirable in new employees.) In this chapter, Mary Moran describes how goal setting helped stretch the future orientation of a group of students who had received a bright future completely out-of-the-blue when they were in first grade. The only problem was that the students' behavior was undermining their chances to take advantage of this opportunity.

—Michael Ben-Avie

HELPING STUDENTS TO ACCOMPLISH GOALS

Each of us has our own personal idea of what it means for a doorway of opportunity to open. Although the opening is exciting, just knowing that so much is available can be rather scary for some of us and may paralyze others. Yet others may grab it and take it as far as they can. It is the ScholarshipBuilder Program's experience that regardless of how able and motivated a child is to move through this doorway, a skilled, consistently available adult advocate should be waiting on the other side to welcome the student through and act as a guide. For the Houston students, I was just such an advocate, reaching out to grasp the hands of the students, of their parents, and of other adult advocates who were so willing to help.

I began working part time at the Houston Area Urban League in August 1994. The halfway celebration for the ScholarshipBuilder Program had taken place earlier in the summer, which meant that the students had just completed sixth grade. At the beginning, the program had been a picture of promise. To be chosen at random, the students and families felt, was a blessing. Parents stated, "It was hard to believe." "I had been praying for a way to send my children to college; . . . [not long afterward] I was told my son had been picked as a ScholarshipBuilder student." It was a very exciting time for them. When interviewed as a first grader, Edric stated, "I want to be an architect." Patting her right ponytail, Chantelle said, "I guess I will be a lawyer!"

Throughout these first 6 years, the students were supported by very involved adults. Merrill Lynch employees were serving as mentors; the Houston Area Urban League was coordinating with the local Merrill Lynch advisor as well as corresponding with the national offices of the Urban League and Merrill Lynch for updates, and the Houston Area Urban League planned and administered the activities. Students were being tutored, going on field trips, attending summer camps, and having holiday parties. More than two-thirds of the parents were participating in meetings and activities.

Assessing the Need

When I came on board, there were 6 years remaining in the program. All but four students had graduated from sixth grade that summer. A few of the students were working above grade level, but more than half of them needed improvement. The students were happy about the scholarship op-portunity, yet, like most children their age, their perception was that the year 2000 was further away than the calendar indicated.

Several students, full of pride, had shared information about their scholarship with their teachers. After I heard that message a number of times from teachers, I realized that the students first had to understand that (1) they had not received the scholarship yet, but were in the process of earning it, and (2) it was their job to qualify for admission to some of the elite colleges they had in mind to attend. The idea of beginning now to prepare for later just didn't have any meaning for most of them. More than half of the students would be the first in their families to attend college, and they and their families were unfamiliar with the processes and procedures necessary for admission.

I realized that something had to be done to get the students ready. They were good kids, full of capabilities, from families who knew some-thing special had happened to them. Advocates were in place and ready to begin. Now, what choices should be made to create positive changes in the students' attitudes and habits?

Before retiring as the Houston Area Urban League's Director of Edu-cation, Dorothy Lombard had described the program to me as one that needed to devote full-time attention to and increase the focus on the stu-dents' needs. The Urban League also had to improve its own relationship with the schools and families. I read the program mission, past reports, and student records on file. There obviously had been a high level of involvement, but just as obviously, there would have to be even more involvement to make the program meet its goals. Luckily, I was employed full-time in the fall of 1995. This was definitely going to be a full-time task.

In each of the 10 cities in which the program was running, the Scholar-shipBuilder coordinator was responsible for making the program compo-nents function with full impact in order to capture the attention of the students and families. *Documenting the Impact of the ScholarshipBuilder Pro-gram on the Lifepaths of Students* (Ben-Avie et al., 2000) gives a good de-scription of our job. Working 45–50 hours per week, we were expected to:

- Assess the progress of each child
- Develop and implement an academic enrichment plan for each stu-dent
- Document the progress of each student
- Plan, coordinate, and implement activities for students and families in the program component areas (academic enrichment, life skills training, cultural enrichment, parent involvement, and mentoring)
- Provide effective coordination between ScholarshipBuilder students,

parents, community schools and districts, Urban League, and Merrill Lynch

- Assist the Merrill Lynch advisor in incorporating Merrill Lynch volunteers to serve as part of the program
- Manage the program activities budget in cooperation with the Merrill Lynch advisor
- Provide regular reports to the Urban league, Merrill Lynch advisor, and national ScholarshipBuilder administration throughout the duration of the program

Implementing the ScholarshipBuilder Program

At first, the other coordinators and I attempted to recapture the students' and families' attention, enthusiasm, and dedication. We implemented various activities and programs to improve academic performance and social and cultural development by 2000. As in life in general, urgent academic and family situations (e.g., school suspensions, danger of failing, poor attendance, and ill health in the family) interrupted the focus of enrichment plans from time to time. Coordinators and program administrators soon realized it was inevitable that these life interruptions would take precedence over our plans. During national conferences given by Merrill Lynch and the Urban League, coordinators discussed these matters in between workshops conducted by speakers who provided resources and addressed problem situations. We were then able to create program ideas to provide more encouragement for the students and ourselves. Coordinators also communicated by telephone. Houston's Merrill Lynch ScholarshipBuilder advisor Joyce Fox, current Urban League education director Jan West, Houston Area Urban League president Sylvia Brooks, and the Urban League Guild took the lead in involving themselves and others to advocate in any way possible.

The ScholarshipBuilder coordinators were responsible for direct service to the students. It was imperative that we evaluate our situation and come up with the most effective options to consistently impact the students. The tools we chose would have to encompass the students' academic, social, and emotional lives. Ultimately, our program activities came to encompass a wide range of activities. Students had opportunities to attend plays and sports events; attend seminars and workshops on writing, public speaking, and etiquette; attend summer camps; and plan and participate in award ceremonies. In preparation for graduation, the students were able to receive SAT/ACT prep classes, intern at Merrill Lynch and the Urban League, participate in rap sessions, raise funds for a college tour across the country, go on retreats, and attend summer precollege programs. "[The]

ScholarshipBuilder program . . . made me focus on even going to college," one student stated (Ben-Avie et al., 2000, p. 13).

We held parent meetings bimonthly. Families used their time and abilities the best way they could. Parents and guardians participated by attending meetings, volunteering as chaperones, assisting with car pooling, participating in programs, and, in their children's senior year, decorating for events. Parents shared information, motivated each other, and attended an overnight retreat. For the college tour, their fund-raising expertise was invaluable.

Developing the Goal-Setting Curriculum

The summer before the students' freshman year in high school, I was shown a copy of agenda planners for students, which were available at minimal cost. Each year's planner was ideally designed for the students' grade level. They were already a part of the curriculum in two students' schools. Easy reference guides were in the front of each planner, and study tips, positive quotes, jokes, and attractive pictures were scattered throughout. I liked them, and I ordered them. In addition, Jan West was using the book *Time Management* by Robert M. Hochheiser (1992) with some young people in one of the Urban League's summer leadership camps. I thought both items would be excellent for the students to use in their high school years.

In a discussion with Judy Allen, a friend from our children's preschool days, I discovered that she was doing something that would benefit the students: She was teaching people how to set and achieve important goals. I began to think that, rather than just give the students the book and agenda planners, if someone could instruct them on using the planners and the principles presented in the book, that would be best.

Therefore, an introduction to goal setting began that summer during a week-long, back-to-school session that consisted of 4 days of academics (math, English skills, and goal setting) and 1 day of fun. Retired Navy Captain Caliph Johnson, then associate dean of the Thurgood Marshall Law School at Texas Southern University, was at the helm of the goal-setting segment. It was a bon voyage of sorts, with ambitious goals in place for the participants. I can recall the length to which Mr. Johnson went to provide visually pleasing and colorful naval vessels, symbols of flags, and the like, on detailed little booklets discussing the steps and strategies of goal making. Mr. Johnson did not require that he be paid for the days he met with the students. The reason that he volunteered was to make his point to the students that they needed to make plans in order to take the voyage into high school—just as sailors must map out their course when making a sea voyage. This was the students' introduction to plans, agendas, and goals. He challenged the students to become seajammers, in the spirit of ancient mariners. Some days he used mood music of bird sounds and water and also one of his favorite books, *Jonathan Livingston Seagull* (Bach, 1973). These metaphoric voyages were symbolic of removing fears and replacing them with courage, plotting the path, guiding the ship (self-discipline), and staying on course.

Mr. Johnson capitalized on the opportunity to capture the attention of the 15 students usually in attendance. He was getting them ready for the 4 years ahead, and I was so excited because this was what I wanted for them. I admired the tradition he had set with his law students of giving each class a name, such as Seajammers, Screaming Eagles, Star Shooters, or Rainbow Riders, which gave them a sense of camaraderie and cohesive identity. He chose Seajammers for the ScholarshipBuilder students because the sea requires imagination and stimulates a sense of adventure and, of course, challenge. To arrive at and enjoy destinations meant defining choices, planning expeditions, and exercising plans with discipline and skill. The students, on the other hand, did not respond to the presentation with enthusiasm, although they demonstrated an understated and respectful appreciation.

Not long afterward, Allen and I set up a meeting at which I showed her a list of the study, time management, and organizational skills the students needed; starting at square one, they needed just about everything. Thus, the ScholarshipBuilder students began their last 4 years in the program with a specially tailored, formal curriculum in goal setting.

We informed the students that they were to participate in sessions concentrating on planning and follow-through and that these sessions would be a part of their lives twice a month for the next 4 years. We had already informed the parents about the need and value of goal setting, and they had agreed at least to try it. We showed them a sample of the agenda planners on order for the students, and they told us which days and times were best for getting their students to the sessions. The only matter not quite nailed down was a temporary site at which the sessions would take place. Students were too young to drive, so transportation was a problem. Tutoring and goal setting initially were held at a police precinct closest to the neighborhood of most students, but a student's grandmother convinced the neighborhood library to allow us to hold weekly sessions there, even though their practice was to offer community groups meeting space only once or twice a month. The library was close to one of the high schools and the neighborhood of most of the students. During the students' junior and senior years, goal setting took place at the Houston Area Urban League office, which was a little farther away, but by that time some students were driving and overall transportation was not such a big problem.

The first few Saturday sessions were well attended, meaning about 10 students participated, but they were not convinced that this goal-setting stuff was worth getting up on a Saturday morning in time to spend from 10 a.m. to noon on it. This concept was also difficult for the parents, who regularly commented that Saturday mornings were already full of errands and personal obligations. This was an ongoing challenge; however, with support from the team of students, parents, and facilitators, success was forthcoming.

Allen and Ross Cahee (another facilitator, who is the principal of M. R. Woods Alternative School in the Fort Bend Independent School District) took time at the beginning stages and throughout the program to develop a personal connection with the students. Sometimes this meant time with students outside the paid sessions on Saturdays. (Allen telephoned or made one-on-one appointments with students when extra attention was needed.) Students participated, and listened, but their hearts were not always in it. Some Saturdays, of course, were better than others.

I was convinced that the activities were just what the doctor ordered, so we hung in there. When one or two students came in, it seemed to verify to the others that they needed to be there. The attendance basically held steady at eight students, although sometimes we had as many as 13 and on a few occasions we had as few as four. All sessions were conducted as if there were a full house, with an agenda in place, goals set forth, and an evaluation of previously set goals.

We had hoped that the students would carry their agenda planner with them all day and go to sleep planning for the next day. That did not happen. The students were told to bring the planners to goal-setting sessions so that the facilitator could take a look at what they had written and done. Allen states, "It had never been discussed with them that you have to plan things or they just won't happen. That was a switch for them." While at goal setting, they were encouraged to plan by recording all school activities, parties, athletic practices, and events so that realistic study schedules could be planned. But the only students who brought the planners were the students who were using them, and these were not as many as we had hoped. "Goal setting was a challenge," Allen states. "I think the challenge was more than just getting up on a Saturday morning, and being there. The challenge was also to become committed to setting goals."

After a few sessions in which they got the feel of our intentions, the students who came began reporting on the positive results of their short-term goals. As the months passed, some students raised their grades in school. Most realized that last-minute preparation was usually inadequate, but that working consistently on small parts of a larger task could be very effective. They also learned that, in addition to libraries, knowledgeable people were available who could help them. One-on-one tutoring was arranged for the short or long term, as needed. In addition, the Internet was now available to them not only at school but also at the Houston Area Urban League office.

After the first semester of their freshman year, the participating students stated that although they had not consciously realized it when the goal-setting curriculum started, they now recognized that planning made a difference in improving grades, that writing down steps made an assignment more manageable, that finding out ways to talk to teachers helped to build a better rapport with them, and that learning new skills was helping them solve problems. Problems did not have to fester and grow. Even though students were not elated, they had found a way to make things work for them. They were coming to sessions with improved grades on tests and with assignments turned in, and they were following up on teacher conferences and visits to the counselor. These signs encouraged us.

At the end of the Christmas holiday in January 1997, when the students were in the middle of ninth grade, about 17 students, facilitators Allen and Cahee, two parents, and I took the students to a university about an hour away for a day-long math workshop. The students were looking forward to seeing and being on a university campus. Before taking the trip, students were made aware that the math workshop was to build on and sharpen their math skills. They were also to be exposed to various testing strategies. The students did not know it, but for those who were ready for the challenge, it was a possible beginning of periodic visits to the university for preparation in math, the most requested subject for tutoring.

However, once they were seated at the desks of college students, something unexpected happened. For the most part, the students did not give this experience the focus and effort it deserved. Immediately, a few of them became sluggish, some conversed among themselves, and when the going got rough, they started joking around. Although the workshop was not a complete failure, the students did not seem to gain what could have been the beginning of a long-term partnership and strengthened math skills.

After that experience, in addition to feeling that the students needed room to mature, the adults felt there was more to accomplish than seemed possible in the few years ahead. Allen took on the job of reprimanding the students that day. The reprimand included our level of expectations for their behavior, the expectations that they would have taken advantage of the experience and the wealth of knowledge the teacher was willing to share for their benefit. Cahee addressed appropriate behavior with the male students. My frustration silenced me. There I sat, simultaneously upset about their behavior and feeling rather sorry for the "put down" they were receiving. I was thinking, "What should I have done to better prepare them?" I realized that such a workshop on a university campus may have been beyond their social and emotional readiness. Young people have a way of telling you things through their behavior.

I drew on my background as a parent, elementary education teacher, parent advisor, business owner and manager, and, most recently, teacher of English to hearing-impaired high school students for 2 years. Those experiences had taught me that young people need well-managed, consistent, and positive activities with clear direction. So we continued, believing that changes would happen only with consistent practice. We stuck with the program.

GOAL SETTING AS THE HIGH ROAD OVER "THE HOLE"

To understand why goal setting is such a critical activity, consider the metaphor of the pitfall and the hole. For most of us, a pitfall is a mere blip on life's journey. For students, a pitfall is an actual hole into which they can fall and from which they may never emerge. No matter how able they may be, some students can be drawn to the hole, which has amazing width and depth and very steep and slippery walls. It is a danger to all parts of our society, and students who fall into that hole sometimes get stuck there for life.

The hole is not the place we want our children to stay or even explore. But it can be very daring and exciting—very attractive from the outside and very gratifying in the short term—so some young people perceive it as the place they want to be. Others perceive the hole as the only place they can go. When they are able and fortunate, young people who fall into the hole bounce right out again, unfazed and unscathed. But all too often young people fall into the hole and are completely absorbed by it. They even forget what life aboveground looks like. The hole is their answer to negligence, poor self-esteem, drugs, undernourishment, low academic achievement, and family problems—all of which are significant blocks to healthy growth and development. The pain relievers of choice are usually drugs and alcohol, which lead to dropouts, more serious family problems, teen pregnancy, disease, or early death.

Parents and educators would like to think that students know the hole is there, that they realize it will only distract from their intended outcome, and that they are able and willing to avoid it. That is often not the case. All students need advocates to show them how to avoid the hole, how to travel far above it on a road that leads to success as lifelong learners and full members of society.

That high road is paved with tasks organized in time. And learning how to pave that road—in other words, learning how to set goals and achieve them—requires both personalized training and ongoing support. In *Finding Fish*, Antwone Fisher (2001) states, "[My experience as a foster child] was a reminder of how fortunate I was that whenever I was really heading toward trouble, each time a guiding hand or an opportunity had steered me away" (p. 306).

For some students, the dream of attending college—although far off in the future—is something they can see for themselves. What supports these students to dream, to initiate, and to take action the way they do? Their families? Schools? Churches? Mentors? Community organizations? Businesspeople who are partners with the school? All of the above.

THE VALUE OF ADVOCATES

Various kinds of advocacy had been available from the ScholarshipBuilder Program from its beginning in 1988. Consider the role of the Scholarship-Builder partnership in the life of J.D.

In elementary school, J.D. was an average to below-average student. If any student would have to struggle to graduate from high school, it would be J.D. But the strong family encouragement to take school seriously, graduate, and attend college was significant. With that support, what this family needed in order for J.D. to graduate was to know what steps to take.

There was ongoing intervention for this student. J.D. would not have taken advantage of some of the workshops, tutoring, goal setting, test prep, college tours, rap sessions, college prep, and so forth, had it not been for his mother and the influence of his ScholarshipBuilder peers. His mother was instrumental in seeing to it that he participated in as many activities as possible, and the program was instrumental in providing the information and procedures. His mother depended on information from the program in order to know which decisions she should make. The other students expected J.D. to attend the various activities, and they encouraged him.

J.D. briefly visited the hole. The involvement of family and the ScholarshipBuilder Program was supportive enough to help him find his way out before negative events compounded. When problems with school arose, the program was notified. Through telephone conferences, suggestions were given to J.D.'s mother about what was important to consider when making decisions at the school. School administrators were alerted or reminded about the opportunity ahead for J.D. and how each decision would affect his future. Eventually a cooperative effort was made and J.D. stayed in school, graduated with better grades than expected, and presently is attending an out-of-state university.

The case of J.D. demonstrates the value of having advocates in place. How many scenarios could have led J.D. into directions far away from high school graduation and all that is involved in acceptance into college?

Along with tutoring, the component of goal setting was the most consistent ScholarshipBuilder Program activity in Houston. It was one of the strongest links to everyday school responsibilities and intervention that the program made possible. This component allowed the adults to have an idea of what the scholarship opportunity meant to each student at each point along the way. The students' attention to preparation indicated the extent to which they accepted the responsibility and also the level of their skill as they attempted to fulfill their own promise. When students were not accepting of their responsibility, the adult advocates had to step in to make a greater effort. The case of R.N. is an example of this.

R.N. began his early school years on track. In middle school, his grades began to fall. Because the ScholarshipBuilder Program had resources in place, upon learning of the student's needs, a mentor came to his aid by tutoring him after school. Assistance from his mentor helped to save the semester. Summer school and regular tutoring were in place for issues bound to take place in the near future. With support and regular parent conferences that lasted throughout the high school years, many measures were visited and revisited just to get R.N. to visualize the possibility of graduating. Meetings with principals, counselors, teachers, family members, and the student himself continued in order to help him get to what he visualized in his future. It was very tough going. In the end, however, R.N. completed the GED requirements, which initially he felt were out of his reach. He had a reason to persist and he did.

It is amazing how quickly a situation can become toxic. Unchecked, one small problem often attracts other, more serious problems. If left unsupported, a child can have a completely different life due to an adult failing to intervene soon enough. At the outset, problems are manageable, which makes solutions easier and more possible. Many people are so quick to say, "It's too late; they are too far gone," as if things were irrevocable, instead of just being more difficult. That kind of thinking frees us from becoming involved. In addition to the personal rewards that come from committing to the intervention, the act of intervening helps youth make positive choices that increase their chances of bridging the hole and achieving positive outcomes.

The group's cohesiveness also seems to have increased the chances of success. Allen commented, "The cohesiveness came with the consistency of the goal-setting curriculum and the students' confidence level—they would share their success stories, and they accepted each other." This is really what we wanted to happen. We wanted them to feel that getting together in the way they were doing does build confidence and skill level. Our consistent presence added to the cohesiveness. As Allen said, "We were always there. It didn't matter if only one of them needed us: We were just there. The program was like a second home to them. All we needed the students to do was just to come in and take what we had to give. The consistency and the confidence level, I think, gave the children a lot of stability. They knew what they were supposed to do during the week, even if they weren't at a particular goal-setting session, because the routine was basically the same." The students came to lean on each other, they had expectations of each other, and they wanted to hold each other accountable for fulfilling their responsibilities and making it.

REAPING THE REWARDS OF PERSEVERING

During their sophomore year, we asked the students whether we should order planners again. The girls wanted them, but the boys for the most part were not enthusiastic. Cahee found out that the boys thought the planners were too big, but since it was important to continue to try, the next school year we got the boys over-the-counter agenda planners that could fit in their back pockets. Nonetheless, there was no evidence that they used them any differently. For junior year, all the girls and the boys who asked for them received planners. For senior year, everybody received one. We didn't ask for their opinion, and we didn't accept their rebuttals. It was evident that most seniors used their planners.

The first 2 years of goal setting gave the students a chance to learn how to set long- and short-term goals; to learn that goals could be accomplished taking small, deliberate steps; and to learn that academic, personal, and financial planning had a place in their life. In addition, sessions focused on exercises to determine learning styles, strengths, expectations, test preparation, use of body language, and improving attitudes as they related to planning for the future.

During the students' junior year, the curriculum placed more emphasis on accomplishing set goals within the 2-hour sessions; for example, requesting a college application on line or by letter, addressing envelopes so that they were ready to be stamped and dropped in the mailbox, or drafting a college essay. If Kesha's goal was to write a rough draft for her English literature class, she did it during the goal-setting session, with guidance available when she needed it. If she didn't finish during the session, she was able to continue, knowing she was proceeding in the right direction. Students ended each session having completed something essential to reaching their goals.

In the students' senior year, sessions focused on test preparation, practice test taking, continuing to establish contacts with colleges, and gathering and completing applications. Our goal-setting sessions now had a changed format. Since it had become clear to the students what and how to plan, we made sessions into time in which students could achieve short-term goals. The students used the Urban League's computers to complete assignments, and they wrote letters to colleges. Because writing skills overall needed some work, each student was required to complete an essay, whether a college required one or not. Essay writing as well as resume writing occupied much of goal setting during senior year. Allen commented, "You could see who had claimed ownership of the curriculum when we did the essays for college. They had a lot of planning to do. Whoever had been consistent with goal setting found it less difficult. We made filling out college applications a process during goal setting, rather than let the students take the applications home and complete them there. But because we had gone through this process during goal setting, they were able to get through it with guidance."

Even when a college did not require an essay, writing one provided the students with "one in the pocket," as well as experience in responding to the type of questions that colleges ask during the admissions process. Also, individuals or groups of two or three students made appointments with me to work with more concentration. It was critical for students who were having a particularly difficult time writing to have individual and/or peer-group attention. By the time the sessions were over, students had evidence of what they had done. Letters were addressed and ready to be mailed, and assignments were completed or on their way to completion.

On college application day, January 15, 2000, 10 volunteers helped the students draft their college applications. I had prepared a checklist for each volunteer to complete as they worked with the students. The checklist indicated what the student still needed to accomplish in order to mail each completed application. Within a week, one-on-one appointments began (with a parent present approximately 50% of the time) to review the tasks with the students and to answer questions. Each student received a copy of his or her "to do" list in order to finish the application process. For example, a "to do" list may have consisted of (1) set goals and action steps to complete them, (2) schedule appointment with school counselor, (3) review grades and required graduation credits, (4) register for the SAT/ACT, and (5) write essay or personal statement.

There were immediate outcomes of our structured curriculum on goal-setting in Houston: (1) The students had a chance to see for themselves how the goal-setting process worked; (2) they had a safe environment in which to succeed and fail; (3) they tended to apply to colleges in a timely manner; (4) they became more comfortable discussing themselves in a group session and receiving feedback; and (5) their independence was nurtured because they could not rely on the coordinator to provide them with magically completed college applications. They had a significant, responsible, reasonable role in the entire process.

After the final celebrations in June 2000, it was decided the final goal-setting session would end as it began, with a bon voyage. This time, however, the voyage was a real one. Allen carefully made preparations for us to take a cruise on a spiffed up boat. In attendance were approximately 15 students (which was considered a respectable number), a few parents, Caliph Johnson and his wife Aisha, Dr. Thomas F. Freeman, speech and debate professor and recently honored as the longest-tenured professor at Texas Southern, Jan West of the Urban League, my son Yuri, and his wife Tammie. Surprisingly, the students were looking forward to the boat ride. Each student received a sailor hat (a symbol of a life preserver), an anchor (to keep them grounded), and a compass (to steer them in the direction of their goals). We enjoyed a catered "mess" of delicious food. During the voyage, a planned program was in place. After my welcome, Caliph Johnson brought the students from the beginning as Seajammers to the next voyage ahead of them, Jan West gave a good luck presentation, Yuri and Tammie read a very funny and realistic list of do's and don'ts for college, and, of course, Dr. Freeman, as a debate coach, made dramatic, but brief, statements to the students, several of whom would attend Texas Southern in the fall. Kesha, who was one such student, aware of Dr. Freeman's reputation and impressed by his presentation, felt sure enough of herself (as a result of goal setting and other Urban League leadership activities) to introduce herself and to volunteer to join the debate team in the fall. She did. What Kesha discovered later was that her goals could not withstand the demands of the debate team. She withdrew with the intention to rejoin the team at a later date.

The reaction to this experience was in notable contrast to the initial bon voyage 4 years earlier. It was gratifying to see that, this time, the students really understood and appreciated the messages they were being given. Looking back, it proved that students must be prepared before they can receive what they need. In other words, the knowledge gained through plotting the course prepares one to see what actions to take, and what symbols and signs are significant as one sails through to one's destination. If students are not prepared, the signs and symbols they are given mean nothing to them.

One important point to make with parents, educators, administrators, community organizations, business partners—everyone working in the interest of young people—is this: If progress is not being made in what you perceive as a reasonable amount of time, radically changing the program or giving up too soon may be a hasty move. Allowing young people time to develop a new way of thinking and behaving, time to grasp concepts, and chances to fail and succeed can make the difference. In our case, the students got tremendous benefits because we decided to stick with the goal-setting curriculum and simply make adjustments to our approach based on our experience. I attribute the students' eventual sense of control of their lives to goal setting. The students themselves have said as much.

> KENNETH: I never [used to] set goals because I never thought I had to. So now [I know] you need to set goals to motivate yourself to see if you can accomplish them.
> JUANITA: The agenda planners help me to write down what I need to do.
> CHANTELLE: Goal setting helped me manage my time.

Allen said, "I was seeing growth when I saw grades improving, even if it was one letter grade or the numerical equivalent. I was seeing growth when they would satisfy their peers' expectations of them. I was seeing growth when I heard the students discussing their peers out of concern for problems they were having, and out of anger over some choices their classmates had made that were taking them away from their goals. I think those discussions brought the students together. I was seeing growth when I saw the students spontaneously writing goals, knowing that they can organize their life and plan for it. It may not all happen the way they plan, but it's not because they didn't try."

We also saw growth in the parents. Long before the end of the program, all the parents were routinely exercising new behaviors that exhibited the same skills we were teaching their children (for example, following up on counseling appointments, calling the school's office to find out what was going on with their children, coordinating with me at the schools on their children's behalf). These new capabilities and habits surely supported the students as they developed their own abilities to set and achieve goals.

WHAT WE LEARNED

When plans for goal setting were being made, we had no idea what impact it would have on the students, but we were sure that the students needed the skills. From the outset, the idea was for the students to take the skills with them for the rest of their lives. The ScholarshipBuilder Program made such an immense difference in each child's life. Years from now, we will still see the impression it made.

For me, it was a learning experience to witness the many wise and willing individuals who stepped forward when asked, willing and even eager to help. The ScholarshipBuilder Program had its own impact merely by existing. Whenever details of the program were explained and opportunities were provided for meeting with the students, many, many people went out of their way to volunteer or provide opportunities and resources. It was very heartwarming and I will never forget the ScholarshipBuilder experience.

After the students' first semester in college, the opportunity to come together as a group was planned by the new coordinator, Nicki Moore, who invited all the students, parents, the Merrill Lynch advisor, the Urban League president, ScholarshipBuilder supporters, and me to a holiday dinner. I learned through brief conversations with the 14 students who attended that the students had had various challenges to overcome. The challenges had to do with understanding how to activate scholarship funds, how to register for and pass placement tests, how to make a variety of decisions, how to get along with and/or change roommates, and, of course, academics. Although some were disappointed in their grades, all seemed eager to make improvements.

The students seemed happy to be together. I observed a comfort that comes from being together for 12 years. Rejoining the group gave them the occasion to notice changes, exchange experiences, and support each other. There were talkative ones and quiet observers. Parents, too, sat together sharing information on what the first semester had been like for them. The general atmosphere was of feeling good to get back together. Erica had chosen a college an hour away from Houston. When questioned on how she felt about seeing her ScholarshipBuilder peers, she stated, "It was nice to see what everybody did and how they were doing and if they liked their college choices. [I] wondered if they had any regrets." Kenneth, who chose a local college and is living at home, felt "excited and happy to see my friends again."

Later, six students met for a more detailed discussion on what the first semester had been like for them. During that discussion I could see that a transformation had taken place. (Earlier, by the way they had been teasing each other and exhibiting familiar habits, I had wondered how much change had occurred.) As the discussion continued, it became apparent that with each of their challenges, they (1) had solved the problem as best they could; (2) had learned, albeit sometimes at their expense, how the system worked; (3) had understood the mistakes they had made and the effect the mistakes had on their status and future; and (4) realized they had persevered.

REFERENCES

Bach, R. (1973). *Jonathan Livingston Seagull.* New York: Avon.

Ben-Avie, M., Steinfeld, T., & Vergnetti, M. (2000). *Documenting the impact of the ScholarshipBuilder program on the lifepaths of students.* New Haven: Yale Child Study Center.

Fisher, A. Q. (2001). *Finding Fish: A memoir.* New York: Morrow.

Greene, J. P. (2001). *High school graduation rates in the United States.* Center for Civic Innovation at the Manhattan Institute, New York.

Hochheiser, R. M. (1992). *Time management.* New York: Barron's.

CHAPTER 9

A Corporate Partner
in the Science Classroom

Tim Fowler

THE WORLD IS CHANGING QUICKLY, and if our students don't recognize that what they are learning is relevant and empowering, then we as educators are not doing our job. No field has advanced more rapidly in the past 20 to 30 years than that of science. We have moved into a new era of technology development that presents a new set of challenges for educators and curriculum developers. We wish to teach new ideas and concepts, but it has been nearly impossible for the school-based curriculum to match the fast-changing pace of technological developments.

This chapter addresses the following questions: Can we provide students with a more complete picture of new scientific industries by calling upon individuals with a high degree of vision and expertise in these fields? Can students' learning be enhanced outside the school as well as within it? Can this learning experience provide meaningful opportunities that enrich the students' development into mature young adults? How can we maintain the quality and content of what is taught and at the same time provide an education that is motivating and relevant? As we continually reconsider the questions of what is taught, how to teach it effectively, and why is it important to teach it, high technology biology businesses are already beginning to provide meaningful direction.

This chapter outlines some of the benefits of joining the efforts of commercial biotechnologists with the efforts of skillful educators. It describes the experience of several biotechnology companies and schools located in the San Francisco Bay Area and Seattle. What began with the companies reaching out to provide the classrooms and the community with a newly developed scientific literacy, has turned into a new model for science education. Bringing the kids out of the classroom and into the laboratories of working companies is adding a new and relevant twist to how science is taught. This interaction is not only benefiting curriculum development but is also enhancing the students' development. And, as an incentive for industry, the interaction will help educate "tech-savvy" citizens and the next generation of scientists.

THE PROCESS OF PARTNERING

Biotechnology companies are involving themselves more and more in the middle and high school classroom and are reshaping how we teach biology.

This novel collaboration began when the companies found it necessary to educate neighboring communities about the nature of their business and the opportunities new biological technologies can offer human healthcare, nutrition, and the environment. Over time, the biotechnology industry recognized the importance of its involvement in the classroom, where a long-term investment in the future results in future scientists and an educated public. This also sends the positive message to students, parents, and the community that they are worth the investment. Educating children and youth to be socially and emotionally well and to succeed academically is a collective task that adults in children's lives and community institutions must share. Meaningful partnerships involving people who are committed to positive change in children's lives and in their learning can have far-reaching implications for success in math and science learning. Teachers cannot do it alone, but require the support and commitment of partnerships to make significant improvements in students' learning in math and science as well as social and emotional growth.

Levels of Involvement by Biotechnology Companies

Industry can integrate itself in the process of middle and high school education on several levels. The first steps usually are made by dedicated employees who are allowed or encouraged to become involved with schools on company time. Increasing involvement by companies often starts with more formalized tours and can include creating on-site workshops for teachers, resources libraries, and high technology apparatus loan programs. Student internships represent a higher level of involvement, as does the most expensive step: hiring a full-time employee to manage the company's involvement with the schools. Let us look at each of these areas in more detail.

First steps: A few dedicated employees connect with schools. The first steps into the classroom are usually small but have a great impact. A few dedicated individuals, given the latitude to become involved in the community on company time, can have an immediate effect. In-house workshops and ad hoc tours provide high school science teachers with up-to-date information about the latest techniques and trends and also form the first connections between the schools and the company. Materials for new lesson plans and ideas for lab instruction also can be exchanged. Most important, these initial steps identify and introduce key personnel to each other and establish one individual within the company as being personally responsible to be the liaison with the schools. At this point the level of commitment from the company is minimal, although significant progress can be made in providing teachers and students with relevant insights into progress in the biological sciences.

Establishing involvement in education as a company policy. Providing resources to teachers who want to explore biotechnology more deeply requires the companies to increase their level of commitment. Involvement over and above the part-time ministrations of one or two of its employees represents a critical decision point for a company. If management does not buy into the program as a matter of policy, it becomes difficult for dedicated employees to find the time and resources to sustain the relationship, much less develop it further. If management does set such an education policy, educational resources can be broadly grouped into three areas requiring increasing amounts of resource commitment: (1) establish a "meet and greet" program, (2) begin a high school student internship program, and (3) hire full-time education liaison staff.

Establishing a "meet and greet" program. Such a program may include a formal program of laboratory tours specifically aimed at high school educators and their students. These typically consist of an introduction to the company, what it does, and the stages of product development, followed by a walk through the facility to interview staff involved with the processes described in the introduction. These tours reinforce the learning of the basic science and illustrate how the advanced technology fits into a business. Often middle and high schools require curriculum assistance. Some biotechnology companies can provide integrated lab and lesson plans that cover the basics of genetic engineering together with recent developments in technology, for example, genomics, proteomics, and bioinformatics. Biotechnology companies also can provide insight into how science is utilized in and integrated with the development of a product. In addition to large-scale manufacturing and skillful sales and marketing, biological products require regulatory approval and solid legal protection.

Providing students with a window into the biotechnology industry. Establishing a centralized library of resource materials can quickly and easily help teachers learn about developments in biotechnology. Classroom visits by scientists is another method of providing K–12 students with a window into the biotechnology industry. In addition to scientists, presentations from personnel representing other aspects of the business provide a more integrated context for students' knowledge of biology and offer insights into other career opportunities. Yet another way students' learning is supported is through job shadowing, which shows students the connections between fundamental knowledge and the active use of that knowledge in the outside world. Job shadowing also provides students with additional real-life role models. These activities give the students the opportunity to explore the business of science as a future career and orient their thoughts into a larger, business-world context.

Establishing student internships. A biotechnology company makes an even more significant investment in students' learning and development when it establishes a program that places students as interns, each with his or her own scientist mentor. Genencor International is a biotechnology company with 1,200 employees located worldwide. Its main research and development facility, in Palo Alto, CA, is where I administered a program that took high school students and placed them with scientist mentors. I acted as liaison between several high school biotechnology educators and our facility. In addition to internships, Genencor provides tours for high school classes and sends scientists to the classrooms to make presentations. The students were accepted for internships after their resumes had been reviewed and each prospective intern had been interviewed. The students prepared their resumes and prepared for their interviews as class activities.

Because it is important that the exposure to any new learning environment be of sufficient duration for the student to truly incorporate the experience, internships were scheduled for a minimum of 10 hours a week over a 6-week period. During this time each student was given a research project that usually was related to ongoing needs of the project team. Under the supervision of the mentor, the student was responsible for conducting an independent piece of research. Mentors were encouraged to provide students with intellectual challenges, rather than utilizing them in a preparative role. Often this involved interaction with the other project team members to exchange information and ideas during informal contact (and sometimes during more formal group presentations). Thus the students were in a position to observe many things about the way adults work—including that achievements often require continuing and concerted effort. They also could recognize that their own increasing mastery added real value to their team, a recognition that helps people of all ages maintain their healthy sense of self. Furthermore, the internships provided the students with additional caring adults with whom they could establish personal, interactive relationships. Active engagement with other students and the tendency to interact with adults are among a cluster of variables found to be related to academic success and the ability to cope with life in general (Ben-Avie, Brown, Ensign, White, & Sartin, 2001).

It was my experience that given this level of respect and responsibility, the students performed at very high levels. The varied nature of life in an industry such as this makes for an exciting environment in which learning is stimulated by a genuine interest in high technology science and scientists. These interactions and the environment the student interns were immersed in would not typically be encountered by high school students. These student interns could now apply their basic knowledge to real-life situations and have a deeper understanding of basic concepts of biology and how it is related to high tech science and business.

Hiring a full-time liaison with the schools. The most significant fiscal investment for the company is to hire a full-time staff member whose job is to act as a liaison for middle and high school education (a full-time employee in the biotechnology industry costs the employer $250–300K per year in salary, benefits, and overhead). The liaison develops networks with local schools, colleges, and universities; with other biotechnology companies; and with any relevant partnerships and grant agencies, and also develops new ideas about successful programs, their administration, and available resources. An example of a company with such a full-time liaison is Immunex, which is located in Seattle.

Levels of Involvement by Schools

The prospective biotechnology teacher faces a number of questions. What aspects of biotechnology are of interest and relevant to students? What can be effectively taught in the high school biology classroom? Just as biotechnology companies involve themselves to different degrees, to what depth should the biology teacher teach biotechnology? The continuum ranges from simply raising one's own level of awareness of biotechnology, to including several units on biotechnology, all the way to developing the curriculum for a full, multisemester course of study.

First steps: Becoming familiar with a new field. Educators who have little knowledge of recent developments in biology or are unclear how much or what parts of biotechnology to incorporate into their lessons must first familiarize themselves with the science and the business of biotechnology. A good place to start is to seek assistance from industrial and academic sources. If local expertise is lacking, one can obtain assistance online. For example, Washington Biotechnology Foundation publishes a guide at http:// www.wabio.org.

Taking advantage of in-depth self-education and hands-on training programs. Once educators have exploited such resources, they can incorporate small pieces of relevant material into the curriculum. The process begins by the educator learning more about how the biotechnology industry uses science—and, in particular, recent developments in biological sciences—to make products. Educators should evaluate whether such knowledge is interesting and appropriate for the needs of the classroom and school. At the same time, educators can develop contacts with other local teachers with similar interests, with staff at biotechnology companies, and with educational partnerships. Attending appropriate workshops, university or college seminars, and/or touring local biotechnology facilities will both provide information and begin the important process of networking.

To give an example, the Science Education Partnership Program (SEP; http://www.fhcrc.org/education/sep) offers biotechnology workshop programs for secondary school science teachers in Washington State. These SEP workshops are sponsored by the Fred Hutchinson Cancer Research Center and conducted at the University of Washington in Seattle. The goal of SEP is to establish long-term partnerships between teachers and the scientific research community. For 13 days in the summer, teachers work closely with each other, with lead teachers, and with SEP staff to gain skills and expertise in molecular biology. In addition, as part of the workshops, each educator conducts actual research with a scientist mentor in a research laboratory. The program also incorporates time to develop a curriculum project. Educators taking these professional development courses obtain not only continuing education credit but also additional support for their classrooms in the years following the workshops.

Integrating biotechnology into the curriculum. Obtaining access to research kits is a good way for educators to begin bringing biotechnology into the classroom while keeping the cost of laboratory lessons low. During the school year, SEP offers educators who have taken its professional development courses a kit loan program, so students have the opportunity to work with the latest biomedical research tools in their school classroom. The kits contain equipment such as gel electrophoresis boxes, power supplies, microcentrifuges, water baths, heating blocks, and consumables such as restriction enzymes, agarose, and other chemicals.

The next step is to begin formally integrating biotechnology into the existing curriculum. The goals are (1) to raise the level of awareness and interest of the students, school, parents, community, and administration, and (2) to demonstrate that this material is relevant to the development and future of the students. Even a small section on biotechnology formally integrated into the existing biology curriculum presents information on a new and meaningful application for the biological sciences and gives students the opportunity to see the relevance of the basic knowledge they have learned in biology classes. Hopefully, the lessons also will be sufficient to demonstrate to all that the material is useful and worth further exploration.

One can present the material so as to align with state standards. For example, the theory of evolution holds that many generations of selective pressure will generate a population of individuals with certain characteristics. The biotechnology industry uses an analogous process known as directed evolution. Specifically, directed evolution selects for new organisms or products using controlled mutagenesis experiments. The new proteins or organisms are identified by their improved ability to confer a selectable property that enables the organisms to survive. The trick is to align the property being selected with the property of the organism or protein that is of value to the company. In this example, evolution is demonstrated in the laboratory in a practical way and used to improve a process or product.

Creating a full-fledged program in biotechnology. Provided that the students, school, and administration see the value of integrating high technology biology into the school curriculum, it may be possible for the school to establish and offer elective courses in biotechnology. However, making the leap from a few relevant classes to a full-fledged program in biotechnology requires commitment from the educators, school, and local community. In addition, funding such an enterprise is challenging. Sometimes a consortium of schools will pool fiscal resources, buy the necessary equipment, and schedule the circulation of these materials around the participating schools. In some areas, experimental materials, necessary to conduct laboratory classes, are available for loan. One example is the SEP kit loan program mentioned earlier. Another is the High School Human Genome Program (University of Washington, Seattle), which provides equipment and supplies to conduct DNA sequencing in the classroom. The school district's administration also may be able to supply some level of financial support at these early stages.

Ellyn Daugherty is a high school biotechnology teacher at San Mateo High School (SMHS), in California (http://www.smbiotech.com). Her experiences in formulating a biotechnology program illustrate how one can go about establishing a full-fledged biotechnology program, and the value of such a program for students' development. Daugherty's interest in biotechnology began in 1988, when she took a 4-week National Science Foundation-sponsored recombinant DNA workshop at the University of San Francisco. At the end of the course, Daugherty approached the school district with a plan to teach a small, part-time recombinant DNA class to a limited number of students. The school district made several thousand dollars available for the purchase of laboratory materials and supplies. With this money and the knowledge she had gained in the workshop, Daugherty established a small biotechnology class. Interest and demand for this course were immediate and increased over time.

At about the same time, scientists at Genencor began hosting small workshops and seminars for local high school teachers. Daugherty and Genencor scientists met, and together they developed high school labs covering aspects of bacterial transformation and genetic engineering. In 1993, Daugherty, satisfied that a greater interest existed, took a sabbatical and wrote an entire five-semester biotechnology pathways program. In 1994, with the support of the school administration and parents, Daugherty became the full-time biotechnology teacher at SMHS.

The student population at SMHS is extremely diverse (57 primary languages and the full range of socioeconomic groups). Daugherty actively recruits from classes other than advanced placement (AP) or honors. (About half of the class is AP or honors students without her having to advertise the class to these students.) Because of this, her students have diverse ethnic, socioeconomic, and academic backgrounds, and there are roughly equal numbers of male and female students. Daugherty's evaluation and grading are based on attendance, promptness, participation, record keeping, and practical skills. Thus, any student (not just the traditional "high achievers") can earn high marks in her class by mastering those skills that will be of use in college and later life. As a result, a diverse group of students, most having a limited understanding of how this technology relates to prior learning or future orientation, enroll in her class. Students experience biotechnology firsthand, and they focus on the relevance of the new technology of biology and on learning skills for college, work, and later life. It is worth noting that this focus on envisioning the far future and on developing the skills to achieve that future is among a cluster of variables found to be related to academic success and the ability to cope with life in general (Ben-Avie et al., 2001).

Between September 1994 and June 2001, 635 students took the first biotechnology course. In the second biotechnology semester, students are given a job-shadow project. Upon completion of two semesters of biotechnology and 150 hours of lab work, any student can apply for an internship project and work with a scientist mentor at a partnering biotechnology company. By June 2001, 325 students had been placed as interns with mentors. All students are given the chance to learn the connection between the information found in the biology textbook and what is actually happening in the larger world outside school. The impact on the development of those students that are exposed to an internship with a scientist mentor is explored in more depth in the final section of this chapter.

RESOURCES

The number of high schools seeking to teach biotechnology is on the rise, as are the number and types of resources available for the biotechnology educator. Indeed, it is now quite possible to incorporate biotechnology coursework into the syllabus without any direct contact with biotechnology experts. That said, local colleges, universities, research institutes, and biotechnology companies are well organized to provide a variety of hands-on experiences and lesson plans for the budding high school biotechnology teacher. Although it is not my intent to provide a comprehensive review of these resources, I do want to mention the network of partnerships between universities and biotechnology companies in the Seattle area, which nicely illustrates what kind of help is available nationwide.

The Genetics Education Partnership (GEP; http://genetics-education-partnership.mbt.washington.edu) is a group of K–12 teachers, scientists, and genetics professionals from throughout Washington State who are committed to improving the teaching of genetics. This group works on developing guidelines (including identification and evaluation of instructional materials) for teaching genetics concepts in grades K–12 that are tailored to Washington's Essential Academic Learning Requirements.

The High School Human Genome Program (HSHGP), based at the University of Washington Department of Genome Sciences, provides professional development instruction in the field of DNA sequencing and genomics for high school biology teachers. During a 1-week summer workshop, participating teachers are provided with the necessary training to conduct DNA sequencing experiments in their classrooms. Participating teachers from the Seattle area also can borrow the equipment and supplies necessary to conduct DNA sequencing experiments in high school laboratories. The HSHGP website (http://hshgp.genome.washington.edu) is intended mainly as a resource for the teachers and students currently participating in the program, providing them with the most current teaching modules and student activities. In addition, the virtual DNA sequencing unit provides a means for classrooms that are not actively carrying out DNA sequencing to participate in many aspects of the program.

The HutchLab (http://www.fhcrc.org/education/hutchlab) is a biomedical research program for students and teachers that emphasizes genetics, molecular biology, and biotechnology. HutchLab, which also is based at the Fred Hutchinson Cancer Research Center at the University of Washington, offers two programs. The first consists of 6-day summer courses of laboratory experience for students. Typically, two such courses are offered each summer. The second program consists of 1-day workshops in which students and teachers work on biotechnological problems. Several of these 1-day workshops are offered each year.

Finally, the Washington Biotechnology Foundation (WBF; http://www.wabio.org) was founded in 1994 to bring together organizations, companies, academic institutions, and individuals to foster education and build partnerships in the field of biotechnology within the Washington State area. WBF offers a four-workshop biotechnology teaching strand annually at the Washington Science Teachers Association Conference. Participants learn about topics such as curricula and teacher training opportunities, and kits that exist for teaching biotechnology at the middle and high school levels. Each workshop is designed for 20 teachers.

REFLECTIONS ON STUDENT DEVELOPMENT

This chapter highlights the new role of biotechnology corporations in re-shaping how the biological sciences are taught in high schools. Teachers are using biotechnology corporations as a resource for the education and development of their students. However, biotechnology is just one example of how students benefit when corporations collaborate in the process of education. This example is not meant to exclude other industries. Indeed, by substituting a few key words, this chapter just as easily could have featured the electronics or Internet-related industries and their impact on students in physics, math, and social studies classrooms. These collaborative efforts present information in a new way, the business environment provides new settings in which to teach it, and the combination is beneficial to the social, emotional, and intellectual development of students.

As corporate funding and competition drive scientific discovery at an increasing rate, the biotechnology industry recognizes its new collaborative role in helping education keep pace. Because biotechnology scientists work with much of the fundamental knowledge needed by high school students, the students are encouraged to make the connection between the biotechnology industry and the biology classroom. When the students connect with science in the larger, business-world context and can think of themselves as belonging to the future that biotechnology represents, their intrinsic motivation to learn and achieve is stimulated.

High technology corporations provide information to keep the curriculum updated and demonstrate how advances in biology have real-world application. Modification of the biology curriculum in this way makes biology relevant to students and provides an orientation into several possible future careers. Moreover, in addition to using that information, teachers can provide developmental opportunities for their adolescent students. The more connection there is between biotechnology companies, biology teachers, and students, the more potential there is for an impact on student learning and development. Students who take classes dedicated to biotechnology experience an intense immersion that accurately conveys the state of the art in the biotechnology industry. When students find the subject to be interesting and relevant to the future, then the influence on their development can be significant.

The most potent effect on student social and emotional development comes as a result of an integration of the high school classroom and the biotechnology company, which allows students direct access to members of the company staff, their knowledge, research equipment, and laboratory facilities. That corporations are willing to open their doors and, together with high school educators, seek to broaden the experience of high school biology students sends a message to the students, the schools, and the communities that there is a common interest in improving student education and development.

Direct contact with scientists in an environment dedicated to the exploration and utilization of biology is motivational and developmentally significant to students in a number of ways. During their immersion, students are given a project or set of tasks usually related to an active research project. As a result, they integrate into a team environment. Each student engages in research, communicates results, and asks for help when necessary. This is certainly a challenging social and intellectual situation, which is easily modified to suit each student's comfort level. I have observed that most students adapt very quickly to the social challenges and also operate at an elevated level of understanding after only a few weeks of immersion.

Mentor involvement is central to this process because each mentor gets to know the student and his or her capabilities. Would-be mentors should not underestimate the amount of time required to provide the necessary personal and professional support. In addition, students require the latitude to experiment and make mistakes (not necessarily the easiest thing to do in such a high-stakes environment!). Failed experiments are a rich source of learning (for both the student and the experienced research scientist), usually resulting in rapid progress in understanding.

It may be that for some students the out-of-classroom experience presents little new information, but instead helps them to develop the analytic and intuitive skills needed to link classroom learning with new applications. Internships help students master fundamental ideas, and also teach them how to use guesses and hunches to help solve a problem and increase understanding. Schools emphasize acquisition of factual knowledge, which forms the basis for being able to use analytic reasoning or leaps of intuition to find the solution to a problem. However, the question of whether a student intuitively "gets it" is rarely asked, let alone evaluated or graded. It follows that the intern's mentor, or expert teacher, is ideally situated to foster the analytic and intuitive process and perhaps even comment on a student's progress in these areas. Research on whether the student's immersion in an internship of this kind helps form or improve the intuitive process would be of great interest.

REFERENCE

Ben-Avie, M., Brown, W. T., Ensign, J., White, J., & Sartin, L. (2001). *Learning and development among high school students*. New Haven: Yale Child Study Center.

CONCLUSION

Integrating Social and Emotional Development with Math and Science Learning on Every Possible Level

Michael Ben-Avie, Trudy Raschkind Steinfeld, Jacque Ensign, & Norris M. Haynes

ENSURING THAT STUDENTS ARE SUPPORTED in their development is too important an issue to leave to "add-on" programs or to the initiative of the teacher working in isolation. Algebra must be integral to the school day, and so must social and emotional development—and they needn't be handled at different times or by different experts in the school. School communities that promote students' developmental experiences are those that simultaneously address students' social and emotional development and their academic learning. The major theme of this book has been discovering how to refine existing programs so that they routinely address both dimensions at the same time (thereby actually lessening the burdens on overcrowded curricula). This involves attention to each level of relationships that occur in schools, from the systems that involve large groups of people and more than one academic discipline to the systems that exist within each person. What underlies this theme is the need to create partnerships to promote students' social and emotional development and math and science learning.

WHAT ARE THE BEST MODELS FOR PARTNERSHIPS THAT FOSTER LEARNING *AND* DEVELOPMENT?

Many models of partnership were presented in this book. A partnership between a school of education and a high school was described in "Youth Development and Student Learning in Math and Science" (Chapter 1). Two very different corporate partnerships appeared in "A Corporate Partner in the Science Classroom" (Chapter 9) and "Stretching Students' Future Orientation" (Chapter 8). A regional consortium for reforming science education was presented in "Excellence and Equity" (Chapter 7), and a partnership with mathematics educators at a local university to support in-depth learning about mathematics reforms was described in "Connecting with Students on a Social and Emotional Level Through In-Depth Discussions of Mathematics" (Chapter 2). It is worthwhile to pause for a moment to look at the impact of a partnership that was described in that chapter.

In Chapter 2, Zeuli and Ben-Avie set up a contrast between the teacher who most closely approximated the ideals of the reformers (Yarrow) and three teachers from another school district, Riverville. These three teachers did not quite approximate the ideals of the reformers as well as Yarrow— but they had far more impact on those around them. Yarrow had the least influence on other teachers in her school because she worked in isolation and without support from her district. In contrast, Riverville district formed a partnership with a local university to support in-depth learning about the reforms taking place in mathematics instruction. The partnership also established peer coaching in schools in which teachers had the opportunity to observe other teachers who also were engaged in reforming their teaching. Moreover, the district designed a coherent strategic plan for educational change. This contrast between Yarrow's district and Riverville helped the authors understand why most ambitious efforts at school reform leave only a momentary trace.

Sustained educational change occurs when there is a parallel process that (1) does not stay only on the level of the superintendent and the district central office, and (2) does not stay only on the level of the teachers. Teachers who go out on a limb to implement change need the active support of both the district central office and their colleagues. For substantive change to happen, teachers have to feel socially and emotionally safe to explore other teachers' approaches and academic disciplines.

In Chapter 1, we shared information about Guilford County Schools (GCS) in North Carolina. GCS used the Yale School Development Program (SDP) operating system when merging three disparate school districts. The GCS district central office modeled collaboration by creating Comer Action Teams. SDP helped the members of the Comer Action Teams to feel socially and emotionally comfortable with leaving behind their adult agendas in order to multiply the students' opportunities to learn and develop.

In 1997, as GCS was adopting SDP, we observed Western Guilford High School, which that year was ranked number 17 out of the 312 North Carolina high schools.[1] The following is an example of what we learned in our study:

> Instead of studying algebra during first period for an hour and physical science second period, the ninth-grade students at Western Guilford High School in North Carolina have a 2-hour block of algebra and physical science to make the two subjects more clearly compatible. Today, the students are solving a math problem that deals with equations. They have the entire 2-hour period to solve the problem. Both the math teacher and the science teacher are in the classroom interacting with students. Yesterday, the students tackled a problem that was developed jointly by the math and science teachers. The math and science teachers work collaboratively to make sure that the students see how algebra is applicable to science. Recently, the math teacher told Debra Barham, the principal, with a smile, "I think I'm becoming a science teacher." Just a few days earlier, the science teacher had said to the principal, with obvious satisfaction, "I'm becoming a math teacher." At times, the 2-hour block is devoted strictly to math; at other times, strictly to science—the teachers have the flexibility to choose.

Through their collaboration, the math and science teachers were modeling a third subject: the connections that may be made between two academic disciplines and between two adults working well together.

ENHANCING THE MOST ESSENTIAL PARTNERSHIPS: THE RELATIONSHIPS BETWEEN TEACHERS AND STUDENTS

No matter what other members of the community become involved in the lives of students, the most influential school partnerships are the ones between teachers and their students. For these partnerships to consistently encourage positive developmental and learning experiences in students, the teachers must recognize that they are powerful adult role models and so must meet certain essential criteria: They must consistently be at their best. They must demonstrate and encourage reflection as well as quick responses. They must recognize the critical importance of the one-to-one relationships they have with students. They must demonstrate resourcefulness as they help students become increasingly resourceful.

Adult Role Models Must Consistently Be at Their Best

Modeling is a primary way human beings learn and develop, and it is largely an unconscious process (Dilts & DeLozier, 2000). Sometimes, children's role models are not real people, but animated movie characters or even machines. Young children often slip into the personae of dinosaurs or dump trucks, and older children often slip into the personae of karate masters, CEOs, Hollywood stars, and (of course!) university professors. It should be part of the mission of all schools to help students slip into the personae of writers and mathematicians and scientists and poets and educators, and to find rewards in making those personae uniquely their own.

When students take on their models' behaviors and attitudes, they are, in effect, acting as if they had had their models' developmental experiences. It is especially helpful to students, therefore, when teachers—who are available to be modeled for half of each student's waking day—are willing and able to open up their own internal dialogue and talk about why and how they are the way they are. Thus, the students can model not only their teachers' external behavior but also the inner resourcefulness that supports it.

The upside of this habit, as the authors in this book make clear, is the benefit of taking on the appropriate beliefs and behaviors of teachers who consistently demonstrate (1) their enjoyment of teaching and interacting with each other and students, (2) their personal resourcefulness, (3) their own curiosity about and love for their subject, and (4) their openness to new ideas and dissent, as well as agreement. The downside, as the authors also make clear, is the danger to students who model teachers who are inadequate to their task or, worse, inappropriate role models whose communication is unclear, whose lessons are ill formed, whose attitude toward the students or each other is adversarial, or whose expectations for the students (and themselves) are low.

Adult Role Models Must Demonstrate and Encourage Reflection as Well as Quick Responses

In addition to paying unconscious and conscious attention to role models and responding by altering beliefs and behavior, students also pay continuous unconscious and conscious attention to themselves. In doing so, they often get stuck in negative thoughts, feelings, and behaviors that impede their learning and development. Until all the adults in schools are experienced at using subtle and rich models by which to understand and improve this inner experience (see, e.g., Andreas, 2002a, 2002b; Dilts, 1996, 1998; Dilts & Bonissone, 1993; Dilts & DeLozier, 2000; Dilts & Epstein, 1995; Gordon, 2002), they will continue to miss abundant opportunities to help students learn and develop.

Even in something "ordinary" that happens many times a day—choosing whether to raise one's hand to answer a question—the inner experience of students as they perceive and respond to what they are learning, is an often-unnoticed microsystem that is essential to school success. The same person can demonstrate several different habits of perceiving and responding, from being fully engaged and on task to being completely distracted from and unresponsive to what is being taught. Math and science teachers hope that their students will display two important habits of perceiving and responding: (1) paying attention to the lesson and responding quickly, which helps the teacher "cover" a lot of material and prepares students for tests, and (2) paying attention to the lesson and reflecting, which over time is more likely to actually produce mathematicians and scientists.

When students respond quickly, they are likely to be perceived by their teachers as successful. These students often feel encouraged to persevere because they have their teachers' spoken and unspoken high regard. But when students are too inclined to speak, they may be labeled as impulsive and held in lower regard, and overreliance on quick responses can train students and teachers to operate by rote, stifle the making of connections to already learned and yet-to-be created ideas, and raise anxiety about getting things right.

On the other hand, because human experience always is initially sensory, a student can be learning and developing without necessarily being willing or able to describe the experience as it happens. Indeed, for some experiences, adding language too soon during or after an experience may distort it by substituting the spoken description (which is of necessity abbreviated, distorted, and generalized; see O'Connor & Seymour, 1990) for the full richness of the experience itself. However, when students are slow to raise their hands, they may be perceived as uncomprehending or disengaged and may lose faith in their ability to make themselves understood. Therefore, as several authors in this book made clear, teachers often should require that students take the time to reflect before speaking and explore with students the connections they have made. Thus, the teachers will be (1) modeling behaviors that help quick responders develop a patient thoughtfulness, and (2) acknowledging that slower responders are on task.

Adult Role Models Must Recognize the Critical Importance of One-on-One Relationships with Students

Children learn best when adults in schools are caring, competent role models, people who build challenging, nurturing, and supportive learning communities that expect and enable students to be their best socially, emotionally, and academically. Students need to feel safe enough to explore, experiment, make mistakes, and learn from those mistakes. In successful classrooms, the fear of failure in math and science, which often paralyzes students and causes them not to persevere and to give up too easily, is mediated by the encouragement and helpfulness of teachers and other adults in the school and in the home.

One of the greatest models for teachers was Richard Feynman, co-recipient in 1965 of the Nobel Prize in physics for his investigations into quantum electrodynamics. Nowadays, nonscientists who know about Feynman remember him as a member of the 1986 Rogers Commission that investigated the disastrous explosion of the space shuttle Challenger. At the hearings, Feynman—who had developed some of the headiest theories in higher physics and math—actually took out a pair of pliers, a screwdriver, and a C-clamp; disassembled a model of the shuttle's booster rocket joint; removed from it a ring made of the same substance as the infamous O-ring; bent it; clamped it; and immersed it for a while in his own drinking glass of ice water. When he unclamped it, it would not regain its former shape. With this simple demonstration, Feynman brilliantly cut through all the bureaucratic hedging and demonstrated the simple reality behind the engineers' numbers: This material was not designed to be used at the low temperatures at which NASA administrators were insisting it be used. The information on the material's stress tolerances was available in data tables, but it was Feynman's experiment that brought the point home to the whole world (Gribbin & Gribbin, 1997). Gribbin and Gribbin remark about Feynman as a teacher:

> Of all the scientists of modern times, Feynman seems to have been the one who had the best "feel" for science, who understood physics not simply in terms of lines of equations written on a blackboard, but in some deep, inner sense which enabled him to see to the heart of the subject. . . .
>
> A fun-loving, adventurous character like Feynman was attracted to physics because physics is fun, and offers opportunity for adventure. You may find that hard to believe. But what's wrong with the public image of physics is not so much the science itself as the way that science is taught and portrayed. Perhaps Feynman's greatest achievement was as a teacher, conveying the fun of science, and entertainer, providing an image of science that cut right across the stereotypes. . . . When he gave lectures, he brought his audience into contact with nature in ways that they could not achieve on their own, allowing them to see nature differently, in a transforming experience, so much so that often when he explained some subtle point in a way that they could understand the audience would break out into spontaneous applause, even laughter. The physicist Freeman Dyson has commented, "I never saw him give a lecture that did not make the audience laugh," but the laughter stemmed as much

from the pleasure of finding things out as from the jokes that Feynman cracked. (pp. xiii–xv)

Feynman was keenly aware of his role as a master teacher and wrote about teaching and learning in several seminal articles and published lectures. In the preface to *Six Easy Pieces* (1963/1995), his famous lectures on the essentials of physics, Feynman wrote:

> I think . . . that there isn't any solution to this problem of education other than to realize that the best teaching can be done only when there is a direct individual relationship between a student and a good teacher—a situation in which the student discusses the ideas, thinks about the things, and talks about the things. It's impossible to learn very much by simply sitting in a lecture, or even by simply doing problems that are assigned. (p. xxix)

Adult Role Models Must Demonstrate Resourcefulness as They Help Students Become Increasingly Resourceful

The relationship that Feynman spoke of is at the heart of true teaching and is characterized by each person's caring for the other and enthusiasm about the subject matter. This relationship, in which teachers demonstrate their authentic, inspired, and inspiring selves, is fundamentally supported by three intertwined sets of behaviors and attitudes:

1. The consistent habit of demonstrating expert communication and rapport skills
2. The consistent habit of demonstrating an orientation toward positive outcomes, rather than a constant focus on what's wrong
3. The consistent habit of employing a variety of models of change management so that each student can discover and develop specific, personalized ways to become more effective, both in school and in life in general (Dilts, 1996, 1998; Dilts & Bonissone, 1993; Dilts & De-Lozier, 2000; Dilts & Epstein, 1995; O'Connor & Seymour, 1990)

At a minimum, these sets of behaviors and attitudes include the following:

- Competence in a set of widely varied verbal and vocal skills
- Flexibility in a wide range of physical behaviors, including sustained eye contact
- Habits of listening actively and refining one's understanding through well-organized questioning
- Comfort in public speaking in groups of all sizes, as well as one-on-one

- The ability to establish, maintain, and break rapport and the knowledge of when each is appropriate
- The habit of maintaining sensory-based awareness, rather than interpreting and mind reading
- A thorough understanding of the conditions necessary for positive change to occur
- An orientation toward positive, well-planned outcomes that take others' criteria, beliefs, and preferences into account
- The theoretical tools and the observational skills necessary to make positive outcomes more likely (Ben-Avie et al., 1999, p. 50)

HOW CAN MATH AND SCIENCE TEACHERS AND STAFF MEMBERS "ON THE SOCIAL AND EMOTIONAL SIDE" BEGIN TO TAKE ON EACH OTHER'S EXPERTISE AND ATTITUDES?

One take-home message of this book is that the expertise and attitudes that promote social and emotional development among teachers and students can be taught, learned, assessed, and refined. Furthermore, it is essential that staff members "on the social and emotional side" develop a solid grounding in the facts, concepts, and skills of math and science. Someday, we hope, these "crossovers" of expert skills will become part of the standard education of teachers, school guidance counselors, social workers, and their colleagues. In the meantime, these skills can be learned and practiced with the help of the larger community and also in staff development courses that create a partnership between school staff members on "the social and emotional side" and "on the math and science side."

The other take-home message of this book is that in math and science classrooms, the expertise and attitudes described above have the essential purpose of helping students develop the competence to access the community of reflective thinkers, past and present. This competence requires that all math and science teachers develop a rigorous understanding of their own field as well as expertise in instructional strategies. This, too, may be taught, learned, assessed, and refined.

CONCLUDING THOUGHT: BEING WITH EXCELLENT TEACHERS AND BEING AN EXCELLENT TEACHER ARE HIGHLY EMOTIONAL SOCIAL EXPERIENCES IN MATH AND SCIENCE

In 1997, Steven Chu of Stanford University was co-recipient of the Nobel Prize in physics. Having heard him speak warmly about his math and science teachers in a radio interview, one of us called his office, and he graciously took the time to talk. When asked to describe his teachers, he regarded the topic as significant enough to follow up with an e-mail message about it. Chu wrote:

> I was really blessed. My high school physics and calculus teachers were really different. They asked us to ask questions and learn to probe in a different way. Rather than having us memorize a list of facts, they asked us to think about their subjects in a personal way and to question things that didn't make sense to us.
>
> Some teachers try to hide their enthusiasm, and they shouldn't. My teachers showed their enthusiasm and shared it with us. They would say something, and then pause and say, "Isn't that wonderful?! Isn't that great?!"
>
> Teachers should be enthusiastic about what they teach. The students will pick up on the enthusiasm; the subject becomes alive and exciting. In part, teaching is like theater—the lines are important, but so is the delivery. It's exhausting to teach, but there is a real high when you feel that it went well. After I have given a good lecture, I feel great.
>
> Teaching is a calling, and students can pick out the teachers who have that calling.

One can see that, for Chu, being with excellent teachers and being an excellent teacher are highly emotional social experiences that emerge from and also enrich one's very being. His eloquent statement makes us eager for a time in which schools of education devote a significant part of their curriculum to the presentation skills not for content alone but also for each teacher's authentic, inspired, and inspiring self.

NOTE

1. To develop criteria for defining Schools of Excellence and Schools of Distinction, the list of rankings was prepared for the State's Compliance Commission. This list is a public document but not an official report approved by the State Board of Education. Ranking was based on a composite of end-of-course subjects.

REFERENCES

Andreas, S. (2002a, April). *Modeling self-concept*. Model presented at the NLP Center of New York.

Andreas, S. (2002b). Building self-concept. *Anchor Point, 15*(7), 4–13. [see also http://www.steveandreas.com/building.html]

Ben-Avie, M., Haynes, N. M., Steinfeld, T. R., Pitterson, S., Beetsma, D., & Weinzimmer, D. P. (1999). *Intervening in the lives of students placed at risk: An independent evaluation of the Institute for Student Achievement COMET & STAR programs, a school-based academic enrichment and counseling intervention.* New Haven: Yale Child Study Center.

Dilts, R. B. (1996). *Visionary leadership skills: Creating a world to which people want to belong.* Capitola, CA: Meta.

Dilts, R. B. (1998). *Modeling with NLP.* Capitola, CA: Meta.

Dilts, R. B., with Bonissone, G. (1993). *Skills for the future: Managing creativity and innovation.* Cupertino, CA: Meta.

Dilts, R. B., & DeLozier, J. A. (2000). Relationship (pp. 1086–1088), Role model (pp. 1133–1134), and Unconscious competence (pp. 1487–1488). *Encyclopedia of systemic neuro-linguistic programming and NLP new coding.* Scotts Valley, CA: NLP University Press.

Dilts, R. B., & Epstein, T. A. (1995). *Dynamic learning.* Capitola, CA: Meta.

Feynman, R. P. (1995). *Six easy pieces: Essentials of physics explained by its most brilliant teacher.* Reading, MA: Helix/Perseus. (Original work published 1963)

Gordon, D. (2002, April). *Meaningful existence model.* Discussion/demonstration presented at the annual meeting of the Canadian Association of Neuro-Linguistic Programming, Ottawa. [see also http://www.experiential-dynamics.org]

Gribbin, J., & Gribbin, M. (1997). *Richard Feynman: A life in science.* New York: Dutton.

O'Connor, J., & Seymour, J. (1990). *Introducing neuro-linguistic programming: Psychological skills for understanding and influencing people.* London/San Francisco: Thorsons/HarperCollins.

About the Editors and the Contributors

Norris M. Haynes is Professor of Counseling and School Psychology at Southern Connecticut State University and Founder and Director of the Center for Community and School Action Research. Before joining the full-time faculty at Southern Connecticut State University, he was Associate Professor of Psychology, Education and Child Development at the Yale Child Study Center and Research Director of the School Development Program. He was also a member of the faculty in the Department of Psychology and a faculty member of the Bush Center. Dr. Haynes contributed significantly to the SDP's training and dissemination activities, designing the dissemination plan and developing and preparing grant applications in support of the SDP's national dissemination strategies. He is the author or co-author of over a hundred publications, including seven books.

Michael Ben-Avie directs the Impact Analysis and Strategies Group, Yale Child Study Center. The Impact Analysis and Strategies Group studies corporate, nonprofit, and government partnerships. The group's purpose is to contribute to the national discourse on how these partnerships may promote the learning and development of children and young people. Studies take different forms: Some are summative and evaluative; others provide ongoing information that the partnerships use to increase the effectiveness of their models. All of the studies produce rich data on which policy makers and funders may base investment decisions. Ben-Avie has co-edited *Rallying the Whole Village* and *Child by Child* with James P. Comer and colleagues.

Jacque Ensign is Associate Professor of Teacher Education at Seattle University where she teaches multiculturalism/diversity of education, and psychology of education in a master of teaching program. For 5 years, in the study she describes in her chapter, she worked with teachers in one of the original Comer schools in New Haven, Connecticut. Her articles and presentations on culturally connected teaching and homeschooling stem from her 15 years teaching kindergarten through tenth-grade students in underfunded urban and rural schools, and 9 years preparing teachers in teacher education programs for urban schools on the East and West coasts.

Nadine Bezuk is a professor of mathematics education at San Diego State University, where she also serves as Director of the School of Teacher Education. A former mathematics teacher at the elementary, junior high, high school, and college levels, she has co-authored materials to help parents help their children learn mathematics and to help teachers help all their students understand mathematics.

Judy Bippert is a member of the Yale School Development Program National Faculty. With San Diego City Schools, she presents the Comer Summer Training Institute each year and recently directed a Curriculum and Instruction Master's Program focusing on the Comer SDP. She is a credentialed teacher with experience teaching junior high school mathematics and currently is a full-time faculty member at San Diego State University where she teaches mathematics methods to preservice teachers and is Field Experiences Coordinator.

James Dolan is Professor and Chairperson of the Physics Department at Southern Connecticut State University. He received his bachelor's degree from St. John Fisher College and began his teaching career as a public high school teacher in Hilton, New York. He received his master's degree and Ph. D. in solid state physics from the University of Connecticut and has taught at Trinity College in Hartford. His research interests are laser spectroscopy and fiber optics. He teaches optics and inquiry-based elementary physics at the undergraduate level and graduate courses in inquiry-based science education.

Tim Fowler has a Ph.D. in molecular biology and is currently obtaining a master's in teaching at Seattle University. He was employed by Genencor International from 1988 to 2000. During this time, in addition to his duties as a research scientist and project manager, he served as liaison with several local high schools and ran the company high school intern program. To date 40 high school students have been placed with mentors at Genencor.

Dionne J. Jones, an educational psychologist and adjunct faculty member at the University of Maryland University College, Adelphi, Maryland, has worked as a senior research scientist for more than 20 years, managing a variety of research projects in public health. Dr. Jones was managing editor of *The Urban League Review*, a semiannual policy research journal of the National Urban League, and of newsletters for professional associations, including the American Educational Research Association. She has authored several publications, including a monograph entitled "High-Risk Students in Higher Education: Future Trends."

Mary L. Moran, former coordinator for Houston's ScholarshipBuilder Program, is currently parent advisor for hearing-impaired infants. Motivated by the ScholarshipBuilder students to pursue further education, she is seeking a master's degree in urban education.

David Pettigrew is Professor of Philosophy at Southern Connecticut State University. He has served, since 1992, as coordinator of systemic reform efforts in mathematics and science for the university, including Connecticut Department of Higher Education Dwight D. Eisenhower Professional Development Program projects. In 1996, he served as the first "Distinguished Professor in Residence" for the Connecticut Academy for Education in Mathematics, Science & Technology, an agency created by a National Science Foundation Statewide Systemic Initiative grant. Pettigrew teaches philosophy of education, as well as philosophy courses for philosophy majors.

Veronica A. Roberts is a senior research associate in the Division of Educational Accountability for the District of Columbia Public Schools. She has oversight responsibility for the research and evaluation functions. She also prepares research/evaluation briefs to inform stakeholders and/or policy decision makers. Her research interests include the designing, planning, and preparation of research and evaluation studies with a focus on the investigation of school-related variables that predict student academic success.

Loleta D. Sartin is Director of the Developmental School Program at Drury University in Springfield, Missouri. She coordinates the collaboration between Drury University's School Development Program and the Springfield Public Schools Partnership. Sartin has served as a consultant for school districts and colleges of education regarding the implementation of the School Development Program Model. She has taught at both the public school and the university level. Her current research interests include university/school partnerships, school reform, and reviving urban education. Sartin received her M.Ed. from Drury University and is currently completing her Ph.D. at St. Louis University.

David A. Squires directs the SDP Balanced Curriculum Process for the Yale School Development Program. His interests center on how school and district management interact with instructional improvement and human development.

Trudy Raschkind Steinfeld is a research associate at the Impact Analysis and Strategies Group, Yale Child Study Center, and an education staff developer and group facilitator. She is also a certified trainer of neurolinguistic programming (NLP) and a member of the training and therapy staff of the NLP Center of New York, in Manhattan, where she teaches NLP and Ericksonian hypnosis. Ms. Steinfeld is a co-author of several research instruments and book-length reports, published by the Child Study Center on school intervention programs, social and emotional education, youth development, and academic learning; has been development editor of many academic books on education, psychology, social work, and medicine; and has developed curricula in creative writing for elementary school students and staff. She maintains a private psychotherapy practice in Brooklyn, New York.

Jayne White is a professor in the School of Education and Child Development at Drury University in Springfield, Missouri. She teaches courses in child and adolescent development and literacy for secondary educators and supervises preservice teachers involved in Drury University's School Development Program and the Springfield Public Schools Partnership. White has served as a consultant for school districts and colleges of education regarding the implementation of the School Development Program Model. Her research and teaching interests are focused on impacting public policy on the basis of child and adolescent development principles and reform in teacher education. Dr. White received her M.Ed. degree from the University of Missouri–Columbia and the Ed.D. from Oklahoma State University.

John S. Zeuli is a research associate with the Michigan Statewide Systemic Initiative. Zeuli's interests include practical reasoning, teachers' uses of research, and the relationship between policy and practice. He is currently working on case studies of teachers' mathematics and science teaching in light of reform initiatives.

Index